RISE AND FALL

OF THE

SLAVE POWER IN AMERICA.

HISTORY

OF THE

RISE AND FALL OF THE SLAVE POWER
IN AMERICA.

By HENRY WILSON.

VOL. I.

FIFTH EDITION.

BOSTON:
JAMES R. OSGOOD AND COMPANY,
Late Ticknor & Fields, and Fields, Osgood, & Co.
1878.

UNIVERSITY PRESS: WELCH, BIGELOW, & CO.

CAMBRIDGE.

PREFACE.

FROM the closing months of 1860 to the spring of 1865, the United States presented to the gaze of mankind a saddening and humiliating spectacle. Treasonable menaces had ripened into treasonable deeds. A rebellion of gigantic proportions burst upon the nation with suddenness and fierceness. Violence held its carnival and reaped its bloody harvest. Millions of treasure and hundreds of thousands of lives were sacrificed on the wasting shrine of civil war.

During that stern conflict, and since its close, thoughtful men have asked why this Christian nation, with so many ties to bind it together, and with such momentous interests to be imperilled, was rent and dissevered by fraternal strife. Why was the soil of republican America reddened with the blood of husbands and fathers, sons and brothers, and bathed with the tears of wives and mothers, daughters and sisters?

In the lights of the present, it is now more clearly seen that the dark spirit of slavery was the inspiration of these crimes against the peace, the unity, and the life of the nation, and that these sacrifices of property, of health, and of life were the inflictions of the Slave Power in its maddened efforts to make perpetual its hateful dominion. These bitter fruits of the seeds sown in colonial times afford another signal illustration of the truth of the inspired declaration that " righteousness exalteth a nation, and sin is a reproach to any people."

I propose to write a history of the beginning and growth, the expansion and extinction, of slavery; also of the development and extirpation of the Slave Power. This work will be comprised in three volumes of some one hundred and thirty chapters, and about two thousand pages. The first and second volumes will trace slavery and portray its influences from its introduction in 1619 to the opening of the civil war. The third volume will describe that series of measures by which slavery was extinguished and the Slave Power broken, the Union reconstructed on the basis of freedom, and citizenship, with civil and political rights, assured to all. The second volume will be published next year, and the third in the year following.

I have striven with scrupulous fidelity to truth and justice to narrate the facts, develop the principles, and portray the results of this "irrepressible conflict" between the antagonistic forces of freedom and slavery. Although I have borne, for more than thirty years, an humble part in this stern strife, and have been personally acquainted with many of the actors and their doings, I have endeavored to be as impartial as the lot of humanity will permit. Of the actors in the great drama I have not set down aught in malice. Of the living and of the dead I have written as though I were to meet them in the presence of Him whose judgments are ever sure.

To my countrymen I commit this work, on which I have bestowed years of unstinted labor, in the confident hope that it will contribute something to a clearer comprehension of the career of that Power, which, after aggressive warfare of more than two generations upon the vital and animating spirit of republican institutions, upon the cherished and hallowed sentiments of a Christian people, upon the enduring interests and lasting renown of the Republic, organized treasonable conspiracies, raised the standard of revolution, and plunged the nation into a bloody contest for the preservation of its threatened life. I trust that this record will reveal to those who raised voice and hand against their country the true nature and real character of that system they sought to perpetuate at such fearful cost; and to those who were loyal to country and liberty, the magnitude and grandeur of the cause in which they exhibited such faith and devotion, endurance and heroism. I trust, too, that the young men who remember the days of their boyhood, when homes were saddened by the absence of fathers, brothers, and kindred, summoned to encounter the hazards and hardships of the camp and field, will gather something from these pages which will enable them to realize in larger measure the toils and sacrifices offered for the redemption of their country and its free institutions, of which they, under Providence, are so soon to become the guardians.

HENRY WILSON.

February 16, 1872.

CONTENTS TO VOL. I.

CHAPTER I.

THE BEGINNINGS AND GROWTH OF SLAVERY AND THE EARLY DEVELOPMENT OF THE SLAVE POWER.

PAGE

Basis of Slavery. — American Slavery. — Slave Power. — Issues of the Civil War. — African Slave-trade. — Slaves brought into Virginia. — Colonial and Commercial Policy of England. — Slave-trade encouraged. — Colonial Statutes annulled. — Spread of Slavery and Increase of Slave-trade. — Slavery in New England. — John Eliot. — Samuel Sewall. — Action of the Quakers. — Testimonies against Slavery by Burling, Sandiford, Lay, Woolman, Benezet, Wesley, Whitefield. — Emancipation advocated by Dr. Hopkins and Dr. Rush. — Opinions of the Revolutionary Leaders. — Slave-trade denounced by Congress. — South Carolina and Georgia for the Slave-trade. — Articles of Confederation. — Development of the Slave Power 1-17

CHAPTER II.

ABOLITION. — ABOLITION SOCIETIES.

Articles of Association of the Colonies. — Colored Soldiers. — Slavery abolished in Massachusetts and Pennsylvania. — The Pennsylvania Abolition Society. — New York Abolition Society. — Rhode Island Abolition Society. — The Abolition Societies of Connecticut, New Jersey, Maryland, and Virginia. — Character of the Members of the Abolition Societies. — National Conventions 18-30

CHAPTER III.

SLAVERY IN THE TERRITORIES. — ORDINANCE OF 1787.

Public Domain. — Cessions of Territory by the States. — Mr. Jefferson's proposed Inhibition of Slavery in the Territories. — Ordinance of 1787, reported by Nathan Dane. — Adopted by Congress. — Sanctioned by First Congress under the Constitution. — Efforts to suspend it in Indiana. — Blessings of the Ordinance of 1787. — Cessions of North Carolina and Georgia, with Limitations concerning Slavery. — The Mississippi Territory. — Debate on Mr. Thatcher's Antislavery Amendment . . 31-38

CHAPTER IV.

COMPROMISES OF THE CONSTITUTION. — SLAVE REPRESENTATION. — SLAVE-TRADE. — RENDITION OF FUGITIVE SLAVES.

The Failure of the Confederation. — Distress and Discontent of the People. — Assembling of the Convention to frame a Constitution. — Difficulties and Dangers. — Antagonism between Freedom and Slavery. — Basis of Representation. — Debates thereon. — Northern and Southern Parties developed. — Slaveholding Interest successful. — Committee of Detail. — Duties on Exports. — Regulation of Commerce. — Slave-trade. — South Carolina and Georgia demand its Continuance. — The Bargain. — Slave Representation. — Slave-trade to be continued Twenty Years. — Rendition of Fugitive Slaves. — The Compromise. — The Slave Power developed   39–56

CHAPTER V.

PROPOSED TAX ON SLAVES. — FIRST SLAVERY DEBATES IN CONGRESS. — PETITIONS FOR EMANCIPATION. — POWERS OF THE GOVERNMENT DEFINED.

Meeting of Congress. — Proposition to tax Slaves imported. — Debate on the Amendment. — Defeat of the Proposition. — Petitions for Emancipation. — Franklin's Memorial. — Excited Debate. — Special Committee. — Report of the Committee. — Southern Members defend Slavery and the Slave-trade. — Tone of the Debate. — Powers of Congress defined and declared. — Mr. Mifflin's Petition. — Right of Petition violated   . . 57–68

CHAPTER VI.

THE FUGITIVE SLAVE ACT OF 1796. — PROPOSED AMENDMENTS.

Bill for the Rendition of Fugitive Slaves. — Bill passed the Senate, — passed the House. — Petition of Free Colored Men to be protected against it. — Exciting Debate. — Memorial of Colored Men of Philadelphia. — Exciting and Violent Debate. — Disunion threatened by Mr. Rutledge. — Action of the House. — Further Legislation demanded. — Mr. Pindall's Bill. — Amendment by Mr. Rich. — Mr. Storrs's Amendment. — Debate on the Bill and Amendments. — Mr. Fuller's Amendments. — Bill passed the House, — passed the Senate, with Amendments. — House refused to take it up. — Mr. Wright's Resolution. — Bill reported by Judiciary Committee. — Debated. — Recommitted to a Select Committee. — Reported, but not acted on 69–78

CHAPTER VII.

THE SLAVE-TRADE. — ITS PROHIBITION.

Increase of the Slave-trade. — Memorial of the National Convention of Abolition Societies. — Bill reported by Mr. Trumbull, and passed. — Memorial of Pennsylvania Quakers against the Re-enslavement of Emancipated Negroes in North Carolina. — Exciting Debate. — Mr. Sitgreaves's Report adopted. — Mr. Hillhouse's Bill amendatory of the Slave-trade Act of

1794. — Senate Bill referred to a Select Committee in the House. — Reported with Amendments and passed. — President Jefferson recommends the Prohibition of the Slave-trade. — A Bill reported and passed in the Senate. — A Bill reported in the House. — A Debate thereon. — Mr. Sloan's Amendment. — Mr. Early's Threat. — Mr. Sloan's Amendment defeated. — Mr. Bidwell's Amendment. — Death Penalty proposed by Mr. Smilie. — Death Penalty defeated. — Bill recommitted. — Bill reported. — Laid on the Table. — Senate Bill taken up, amended, and passed. — Mr. Randolph's Defiance. — Further Legislation demanded . . . 79-97

CHAPTER VIII.

DOMESTIC AND FOREIGN SLAVE-TRADE. — NEGOTIATIONS WITH FOREIGN POWERS.

Extent of Domestic and Foreign Slave-trade. — Cruel Character of the Traffic. — Slave-breeding. — Prosecution of the Foreign Trade. — Christian Sentiment. — Action of the Quakers. — Motion of Mr. Burrell. — Rufus King. — Mr. Morrill. — Mr. Eaton's Motion. — Mercer's Resolution. — Passage of the Bill. — Mr. Gorham's Report. — Co-operation with Foreign Powers recommended. — Treaty of 1815. — British Proposition. — Mr. Rush's Treaty. — Action of England. — Dilatory Action of the Senate. — Treaty amended. — Mr. Clay's Reply. — Insincerity of the American Government 98-111

CHAPTER IX.

FOREIGN RELATIONS OF THE GOVERNMENT INFLUENCED BY SLAVERY.

American Government humiliated by Slavery. — Treaty of 1783. — Demands on England. — Jay's Treaty. — Free Negroes of San Domingo. — Demands of Napoleon. — Monroe Doctrine. — Congress at Panama. — Report of the Committee on Foreign Affairs. — Debate. — War of 1812. — Randolph's Speech. — Instruction to the Peace Commissioners. — Treaty of Ghent. — Demands on the Commander of the British Squadron. — Position of the British Government. — Persistent Demands of the American Government for Payment of Slaves. — Decision referred to Russia. — Proposed Invasion of Cuba by Mexico. — Intervention of the Government of the United States. — Debate in the Senate. — Instructions of Mr. Clay to the Panama Commissioners 112-123

CHAPTER X.

INDIAN POLICY AFFECTED BY SLAVERY. — EXILES OF FLORIDA.

Disgraceful Attitude of the Nation. — Escape of Slaves into Florida. — Return of Fugitives refused. — Commissioners to negotiate a Treaty with the Creeks. — Action of Georgia. — Protection demanded. — Failure of Negotiations. — Treaty negotiated at New York. — Stipulation for the Return of Slaves. — Spanish Authorities refuse to surrender Slaves. — Misconduct of Georgia. — Claims on England for Fugitive Slaves. — Commissioners appointed to meet the Creeks in Washington. — Annexation of Florida pressed by the Slave Power. — Amelia Island seized by Georgia. — Expedition sent by Georgia into Florida to capture Fugitives. — Raid into Florida. — Negro Fort. — Order of General Jackson to invade Florida. — Negro Fort captured. — Exiles killed, captured, and reduced to Slavery. — Disgrace of the Nation. — General Jackson enters Florida. — Defeats the Indians. — Acquisition of Florida. — Treaty of Indian Spring. — Treaty of Camp Moultrie. — Seizure of Slaves. — Fugitives captured by the Army. — Slave-catchers permitted to hunt Slaves . 123-134

CHAPTER XI.

THE MISSOURI STRUGGLE. — THE COMPROMISES.

The Louisiana Purchase. — Missouri Territory. — Bill authorizing the Territory to form a Constitution. — Mr. Tallmadge's Amendment prohibiting Slavery. — Exciting Debate. — Amendment agreed to. — Inhibition of Slavery stricken out by the Senate. — Bill lost. — Territory of Arkansas organized. — Mr. Taylor's Amendment. — Bill introduced by Mr. Scott to authorize Missouri to form a Constitution. — Maine and Missouri united in the Senate. — Mr. Roberts's Amendment for the Inhibition of Slavery. — Debate in the Senate. — Mr. Thomas's Amendment. — Amendment agreed to. — Bill passed the Senate. — House disagree to Senate's Amendment. — Mr. Taylor's Amendment. — Bill passed. — Conference Committee. — Prohibition of Slavery defeated in the House. — Prohibition of Slavery north of the Parallel of 36° 30' agreed to. — Triumph of the Slave Power complete 135-152

CHAPTER XII.

ADMISSION OF MISSOURI. — ATTEMPT TO INTRODUCE SLAVERY INTO ILLINOIS.

Constitution of Missouri. — Resolution of Admission in the Senate. — Mr. Eaton's Proviso. — Mr. Wilson's Proviso. — Debate. — Passage of the Resolution of Admission. — Report by Mr. Lowndes in the House. — Remarks by Sergeant, Storrs, Lowndes, Cook. — House Resolution rejected. Senate Resolution referred to a Committee of Thirteen. — Report of Committee rejected. — Speech of Mr. Pinckney. — Mr. Brown's Proposition. — Appointment of Joint Special Committee. — Mr. Clay's Compromise adopted. — Conditions accepted by Missouri. — Slaves in Illinois. — Slave Codes. — Governor Coles. — Defeat of the Plot to make Illinois a Slave State 153-164

CHAPTER XIII.

EARLY ANTISLAVERY MOVEMENTS. — BENJAMIN LUNDY. — WILLIAM LLOYD GARRISON.

Aggressive and Dominating Spirit of Slavery. — Elias Hicks. — Antislavery in Kentucky and Tennessee. — Benjamin Lundy. — He organizes an Antislavery Society in Ohio. — "Genius of Emancipation." — Removed to

Tennessee. — Established Abolition Societies in North Carolina. — Meeting of the American Abolition Convention. — Political Action recommended. — Establishes his Paper in Baltimore. — Visits the Eastern States. — Joined by Mr. Garrison. — Imprisonment of Mr. Garrison. — Paper removed to Washington. — Establishes the "National Inquirer." — Removal to the West. — Death. — Character. — Mr. Garrison. — Joins Mr. Lundy. — Adopts the Doctrine of Immediate Emancipation. — Denunciation of the Slave-trade. — Imprisoned in Baltimore. — Release through Intervention of Arthur Tappan. — Denounces the Colonization Society. — Establishes "The Liberator." — Public Sentiment. — Rewards offered for his Arrest. — His Fearlessness, Inflexibility, and Persistency 165–188

CHAPTER XIV.

THE VIRGINIA CONSTITUTIONAL CONVENTION. — SOUTHAMPTON INSURRECTION. SLAVERY DEBATE IN THE LEGISLATURE.

Constitutional Convention. — Struggle between Eastern and Western Virginia. — Slaveholding Interest Successful. — Southampton Insurrection. — Nat Turner. — Message of Governor Floyd. — Resolution of Mr. Summers. — Debate on Slavery. — Proposition of Thomas Jefferson Randolph. — Mr. Goode's Motion to discharge the Committee. — Report of the Committee. — Mr. Preston's Amendment. — Speeches of Mr. Moore, Mr. Bolling, Mr. Randolph, Mr. Rives, Mr. Brodnax, Mr. Daniel, Mr. Faulkner, Mr. Knox, Mr. Summers, Mr. McDowell. — The "Richmond Inquirer." — Reaction in the State 189–207

CHAPTER XV.

THE FORMATION AND PURPOSES OF THE AMERICAN COLONIZATION SOCIETY.

Its Inconsistencies. — Views of Dr. Hopkins. — Mr. Jefferson's Proposition. — Resolutions of the Virginia Legislature. — Judge Tucker's Plans of Emancipation. — Mercer's Resolutions. — Meetings of the Society. — Its Constitution and Officers. — Its Purpose. — Equivocal Position. — Declarations of Mr. Clay. — Avowals of its Advocates. — Views of the "African Repository." — Black Laws. — Compulsory Colonization. — Action of Maryland Legislature. — Action of the Free People of Color. — Views of the National Conventions of Free Colored Men. — Declaration of Mr. Webster. — Mr. Garrison's Mission to England. — Eliot Cresson. — Protest of the British Abolitionists. — Address of Mr. Garrison. — Hold of the Colonizationists upon the Country. — Their Proscriptive Course. — Encouragement to Mobs 208–222

CHAPTER XVI.

NEW ENGLAND AND NEW YORK CITY ANTISLAVERY SOCIETIES.

Conference at the Office of Samuel E. Sewall. — Adjourned Meeting. — Adoption of the Preamble and Constitution of the New England Anti-

slavery Society. — Officers of the Society. — Principles enumerated. —
Address to the People. — First Annual Meeting. — Resolutions. — First
Annual Report. — Mr. Garrison's Resolution in Favor of a National Con-
vention. — "Emancipator." — Great Excitement — Public Meeting. —
Organization of the New York City Antislavery Society. — Arthur Tap-
pan. — Lewis Tappan. — William Goodell. — Joshua Leavitt. — Coloniza-
tionists. — Denunciation of the Abolitionists. — Rapid Increase of the
Abolitionists. — Publications of John G. Whittier, Lydia Maria Child,
Amos A. Phelps   223–236

CHAPTER XVII.

HOSTILITY TO COLORED SCHOOLS. — MISS CRANDALL'S SCHOOL SUPPRESSED.

Slavery Hostile to Education. — Proposed Collegiate School at New Haven.
— Hostile Action of the Citizens of New Haven. — Noyes Academy in
New Hampshire. — Colored Students admitted. — Institution broken up.
— Miss Crandall's School in Connecticut. — Admission of Colored Pupils.
— Hostility of the People. — Arbitrary Legislation. — Imprisonment of
Miss Crandall. — Samuel J. May. — Arthur Tappan. — Trial. — Failure
of the Prosecution. — Persecution of Miss Crandall. — Incendiary At-
tempts. — Abandonment of her School. — Her Opposers Triumphant   237–247

CHAPTER XVIII.

NATIONAL ANTISLAVERY CONVENTION AT PHILADELPHIA. — ORGANIZATION OF THE AMERICAN ANTISLAVERY SOCIETY.

National Antislavery Convention called. — Excited Condition of the Public Mind. — Conference held at the House of Evan Lewis. — Assembling
of the Convention. — Its Officers. — Committee on the Declaration of
Sentiments. — Resolutions. — Speeches of Lewis Tappan, Amos A. Phelps.
— Female Antislavery Societies recommended. — The Constitution. —
The Object of the Society the entire Abolition of Slavery. — Conference
on the Declaration of Sentiments. — Words of Elizur Wright, Jr. — Decla-
ration of Sentiments prepared by Mr. Garrison. — Reported by Mr. Atlee.
— The Declaration adopted. — Signatures to the Declaration. — Its Doc-
trines. — Officers of the Society, Elizur Wright, Jr., John G. Whittier,
Amos A. Phelps, Theodore D. Weld, Ellis Gray Loring, Robert Purvis. —
Increase of Auxiliary Societies   248–263

CHAPTER XIX.

LANE SEMINARY. — ANTISLAVERY ACTION.

Antislavery Debate at Lane Seminary. — Action of the Trustees. — Antislavery Students dissolve their Connection with the Institution. — Offer
of the American Antislavery Society to give the Bible to Slaves. — Conduct of Managers of the Bible Society. — Abolitionists mobbed in New
York. — Address issued by the Abolitionists. — Address of Massachusetts

Antislavery Society. — Doctrines of the Abolitionists. — Abolitionists arraigned in the Annual Message of President Jackson. — Reply of the American Antislavery Society. — Activity of the Abolitionists. — Rapid Increase in Numbers 264–273

CHAPTER XX.

MOBS. — OUTRAGES IN CINCINNATI. — WOMEN MOBBED IN BOSTON.

Proscription. — Theodore D. Weld. — James G. Birney. — Establishment of the "Philanthropist." — Mobs. — Meeting of the Citizens of Cincinnati. — Resolution to suppress the "Philanthropist." — Firmness of the Antislavery Committee. — Riotous Mob. — Destruction of the Press. — The "Philanthropist" continued. — Dr. Bailey. — Mobs in Philadelphia. — Continued Violence against the Abolitionists. — Orange Scott. — George Storrs. — Meeting of Citizens of Boston in Faneuil Hall. — Boston Female Antislavery Society. — Public Meeting of the Society. — George Thompson. — Mob Violence. — Mayor Lyman. — Seizure of Mr. Garrison. — Imprisoned. — Francis Jackson. — Meeting at his House. — Remarks of Miss Martineau 274–286

CHAPTER XXI.

RIOTOUS DEMONSTRATIONS IN NEW YORK AND VERMONT.

Convention at Utica. — Mr. Beardsley. — Joshua A. Spencer. — Hall occupied by Citizens. — Meeting in the Church. — Society formed. — Mob. — Convention broken up. — Members insulted. — Gerrit Smith. — Members invited to meet at Peterboro'. — Officers of the Society chosen. — Resolution and Speech by Mr. Smith. — Antislavery Cause placed on High Principle. — Samuel J. May. — Mob in Vermont. — Mr. Knapp. — Colonel Miller. — Years of Mobs. — Dedication of Pennsylvania Hall. — Speeches by Alvan Stewart. — Mr. Garrison. — Miss Angelina Grimké. — Miss Abby Kelley. — Mob. — Burning of Pennsylvania Hall. — Impotence of City Authorities 287–298

CHAPTER XXII.

SLAVERY AND THE SLAVE-TRADE IN THE DISTRICT OF COLUMBIA.

The Seat of Government. — Sectional Claims. — Capital fixed on Slave Soil. — Slave Codes of Virginia and Maryland indorsed. — Inhumanity of the Slave Laws. — Jails used by Slave-traders. — Randolph's Resolution. — Speech. — Judge Morrell. — Petition of the Citizens against the Traffic. — Mr. Miner's Resolutions and Speech. — Resolutions adopted. — Committee. — Communication of the Grand Jury against the Slave-trade. — Slave-traders licensed by the City of Washington. — Men and Women whipped on their bare backs. — Laws against Free Negroes. — Responsibility of the Northern People. — Arrest, Imprisonment, and Trial of Dr. Reuben Crandall 299–306

CHAPTER XXIII.

PETITIONS AGAINST SLAVERY AND THE SLAVE-TRADE IN THE DISTRICT OF COLUMBIA. — DENIAL OF THE RIGHT OF PETITION.

Presentation of Antislavery Petitions. — Debate thereon. — Petitions laid on the Table. — Meeting of the XXIVth Congress. — Presentation of Antislavery Petitions. — Excited Debate. — Mr. Jarvis's Resolution. — Mr. Pinckney's Resolution. — Report of the Committee. — Petitions ordered to be laid on the Table. — Presentation of Antislavery Petitions in the Senate. — Mr. Calhoun's Motion. — Debate thereon. — Mr. Calhoun's Motion to reject Petitions defeated. — Mr. Buchanan's Motion to reject the Prayer of Petitioners adopted. — Long Debate. — Servility of Northern Members. — The South victorious 307-320

CHAPTER XXIV.

NORTHERN LEGISLATION DEMANDED.

Spirit of the Abolitionists. — Mr. Sullivan's Pamphlet. — Dr. Leonard Woods. — Mr. Hazard's Report. — Charleston Post-office rifled. — Public Meeting. — Conduct of the New York Postmaster. — Amos Kendall's Letter. — His Course. — Report of Mr. Calhoun. — Governor McDuffie's Message. — Resolutions of South Carolina Legislature. — Resolutions of Southern States. — Governor Ritner's Message. — Governor Gayle's Demand for Mr. Williams. — Message of Governor Marcy. — Governor Dorr. — Report of Mr. Stevens. — Failure to legislate. — Edward Everett. — His Readiness to shoulder a Musket to put down Insurrection. — Mr. Cambreleng rebukes him. — His Response to Southern Demands. — His Message. — Referred to a Select Committee. — Resolution of Southern States. — Action of Massachusetts Antislavery Society. — Hearing before the Committee. — Speeches of Mr. May, Mr. Loring, Mr. Garrison, Mr. Goodell. — Mr. Lunt interrupts Mr. Goodell. — Dr. Follen insulted by Mr. Lunt. — Dr. Follen sustained by Mr. May. — Memorial to the Legislature. — Another Hearing. — Speakers interrupted by Mr. Lunt. — Excitement of the Audience. — Mr. Lunt's Report. — Resolutions laid on the Table 321-338

CHAPTER XXV.

INCENDIARY PUBLICATION BILL. — ADMISSION OF ARKANSAS. — CONVERSION OF FREE SOIL INTO SLAVE SOIL. — ATTEMPT TO CENSURE MR. ADAMS. — RIGHT OF PETITION DENIED.

President Jackson's Message. — Referred to a Special Committee. — Mr. Calhoun's Report. — Incendiary Publication Bill. — Debate thereon. — Mr. Van Buren's casting Vote. — Defeat of the Bill. — Application of Arkansas for Admission into the Union. — Constitution guarantees Perpetual Slavery. — Debate on the Admission. — Mr. Adams's Amendment rejected. — Arkansas admitted. — The Boundaries of Missouri extended.

— Free Soil made Slave Soil. — Success of the Slaveholders. — Second Session of the XXIVth Congress. — Presentation of Antislavery Petitions. — Presentation of a Petition by Mr. Adams purporting to come from Slaves. — Violent Scene in the House. — Mr. Patton's Motion to return the Petition to Mr. Adams. — Motion of Mr. Thompson to censure Mr. Adams. — Substitute moved by Mr. Lewis. — Angry Debate. — Mr. Adams's Defence. — Triumph of Mr. Adams. — Speech of Mr. Slade. — Violent Scene. — Caucus of Southern Members. — Adoption of Mr. Patton's Resolution. — Antislavery Papers not to be debated, printed, or read. — Subserviency of Congress 339-354

CHAPTER XXVI.

ACTIVITY OF THE ABOLITIONISTS. — ACTION OF NORTHERN LEGISLATURES.

The Abolitionists hopeful. — Meeting of the Massachusetts Antislavery Society in the Capitol. — Mr. Stanton's Resolutions. — Public Sentiment. — Formation of the Illinois Antislavery Society. — Black Laws of Ohio. — Condition of the Colored People in Ohio. — Hearing before a Committee of the Massachusetts Legislature. — Mr. Stanton's Speech. — Action of the Legislature. — Decision of Judge Shaw. — James C. Alvord. — Resolutions against Texas. — Legislatures of Connecticut and Vermont 355-373

CHAPTER XXVII.

THE ALTON TRAGEDY. — MURDER OF ELIJAH P. LOVEJOY.

Mr. Lovejoy discusses the Slavery Question. — Maintains the Right of the Press and Speech. — Murder of a Negro. — Charge of Judge Lawless. — Destruction of the Office of the "Observer." — The Press destroyed at Alton. — The Slaveholders demand its Suppression. — It is destroyed. — Mr. Lovejoy mobbed in Missouri. — Insulted at Home. — Speech to the Citizens. — Excitement in Alton. — Mr. Linder leads a Mob. — State Society formed at Upper Alton. — Speech of Edward Beecher. — Meeting at the Store to protect the Press. — Assault upon the Warehouse. — The Fire returned. — Mr. Lovejoy shot; died. — Press thrown into the River. — The Murder applauded or excused by the Supporters of Slavery. — Resolutions of the Boston Abolitionists. — Faneuil Hall refused. — Dr. Channing's Letter. — Mr. Hallett's Resolutions. — The Hall granted. — Address of Dr. Channing. — Resolutions of Mr. Hallett. — Mr. Austin's Speech. — Reply of Wendell Phillips. — Excitement. — Action of the National and Massachusetts Antislavery Societies. — Edmund Quincy. — Non-Resistants 374-389

CHAPTER XXVIII.

CALHOUN'S RESOLUTIONS. — ATHERTON'S RESOLUTIONS. — ASHBURTON TREATY.

Calhoun's Resolutions. — Smith's Amendment. — Allen's Motion. — Debate. — Atherton's Resolutions. — Southern Whigs. — Mr. Slade. — Speech of

Mr. Clay. — Speech of Mr. Morris. — Resolutions of Vermont. — Meeting of the XXVIth Congress. — Mr. Wise's Resolutions. — Mr. Thompson's Resolutions. — Menace of Cooper. — Mr. Botts. — Motion of Mr. Adams. — Amendment of William Cost Johnson. — Feeling of the South. — Letter of the World's Convention to Southern Governors. — Quintuple Treaty. — Protest of General Cass. — Ashburton Treaty. — Debate in the Senate. — The Treaty sustained 390–403

CHAPTER XXIX.

DISSENSION AMONG THE ABOLITIONISTS. — DISRUPTION OF THE AMERICAN ANTISLAVERY SOCIETY.

Increase of the Abolitionists. — Dissensions. — New York Abolitionists vote for Seward. — Opposition of Mr. Goodell. — New Party proposed by Mr. Smith. — Action of the Massachusetts Antislavery Society. — Young Men's Antislavery State Convention at Worcester. — Resolution. — Political Action. — The Woman Question. — Pastoral Letter. — New England Convention. — Protest of Mr. Torrey. — Memorial to the Churches. — Action of the Rhode Island Consociation. — Churches and Ministers. — The Abolitionists. — Controversy between the Massachusetts and National Antislavery Societies. — Opinion of Mr. Birney. — Sixth Anniversary. — The Woman Question. — New England Antislavery Convention. — Massachusetts Abolition Society. — Address of the Society. — Bitter Controversy. — Financial Action. — Proposition to dissolve the American Antislavery Society. — Sale of the "Emancipator." — Seventh Anniversary of the American Antislavery Society. — Rights of Woman conceded. — Disruption. — American and Foreign Antislavery Society organized. — Both Societies appeal to the Public 404–422

CHAPTER XXX.

ABOLITION PETITIONS. — ARRAIGNMENT OF MR. ADAMS. — RIGHT OF PETITION WON. — MR. ADAMS'S POSITION.

The Election of 1840. — Death of President Harrison. — President Tyler. — Mr. Adams's Motion to repeal the 21st Rule adopted. — The South warned against the Abolitionists. — President Tyler's Letter. — Thomas F. Marshall, Henry A. Wise, and Joshua R. Giddings. — Vote on 21st Rule reconsidered. — Discussion. — Petition presented by Mr. Adams. — Resolution of Censure. — Caucus. — Mr. Weld and Mr. Leavitt. — Marshall's Resolutions. — Speech. — Mr. Adams's Defence. — Remarks of Wise. — Adams's Reply. — Liberal Action of Underwood, Arnold, and Botts. — Resolution laid on the Table. — Debate in XXVIIIth Congress. — Remarks of Hale and Hamlin. — Rule abrogated and Right of Petition secured. — Position of Mr. Adams. — Criticisms of Garrison, Birney, and Goodell 423–433

CHAPTER XXXI.

COASTWISE SLAVE-TRADE. — DEMANDS UPON THE BRITISH GOVERNMENT. — CENSURE OF MR. GIDDINGS.

Coastwise Slave-trade. — American Vessels wrecked. — Slaves liberated by British Authorities. — Representations of the Case by the American Minister to England. — The Action of the British Government denounced. — Resolutions of Mr. Calhoun. — Debate on the Resolutions. — Remarks of Mr. Porter. — Passage of the Resolutions. — Exasperation of the Slaveholders. — The "Creole" seized by the Slaves and carried into Nassau. — Refusal to surrender the Slaves. — Excitement in the South. — Excited Debate in the Senate. — Mr. Calhoun's Resolutions relating to the "Creole." — Mr. Webster's Despatch to Mr. Everett. — Approved by Mr. Calhoun. — Action of England. — Resolution of Mr. Giddings. — Exciting Scene. — Resolution of Censure by Mr. Botts. — Resolution adopted by Mr. Weller. — Resolution of Censure passed. — Mr. Giddings sustained by his Constituents 439–455

CHAPTER XXXII.

THE "AMISTAD" CAPTIVES.

Demands of Slavery. — The "Amistad" captured by the Africans. — Taken to New London. — Africans claimed as Slaves. — Demands of the Spanish Minister. — Africans before the District Court. — Conduct of District Attorney. — Instructions of the Secretary of State. — A Committee appointed to aid the Africans. — The Attorney-General of the United States. — Africans held for Trial. — Decision of the Circuit Court. — President. — Declaration of the Secretary of State. — Appeal to the Supreme Court. — Efforts of the Committee. — Mr. Adams employed. — His Argument. — Arraignment of the President and his Cabinet. — Discharge of the Prisoners. — Labors of Lewis Tappan 456–469

CHAPTER XXXIII.

THE PRIGG CASE. — THE USE OF ITS JAILS FORBIDDEN BY MASSACHUSETTS. — AN AMENDMENT OF THE CONSTITUTION PROPOSED.

Various Interpretations of the Constitution. — Margarette Morgan. — Prigg Case. — Supreme Court of Pennsylvania. — Supreme Court of the United States. — Decision. — State Legislation not required. — Taney. — Daniel. — Jurisdiction of the Government. — Supreme Court of Massachusetts. — State Laws repealed. — Laws against the Use of Jails. — Latimer's Arrest. — Trial. — City Officers. — Excitement. — Public Meetings. — Meeting in Faneuil Hall. — Edmund Quincy. — Joshua Leavitt. — Disturbance. — Speech of Phillips. — Remonstrances. — Latimer Journal. — Popular Demonstrations. — Grey paid by Mr. Colver. — Convention. — Petition to the Legislature. — Meeting in Faneuil Hall. — Petition pre-

sented to Congress by John Quincy Adams. — Proposed Amendment of
the Constitution. — Petition. — Resolutions of Massachusetts. — Singular
Avowal of Mr. Wise. — Mr. Holmes. — Speech of Mr. Adams. — Report of
Committee. — Massachusetts Senators. — Action of the Legislature   470 - 487

CHAPTER XXXIV.

INTERMARRIAGE LAW OF MASSACHUSETTS. — CASTE.

The Law of Massachusetts. — Petitions. — Report of Mr. Lincoln. — Debate. — Mr. Davis's Report. — Mr. Bradburn's Bill. — General Howe's
Bill. — Sharp Debate. — Repeal of the Law. — Colored Persons excluded
from the Cars. — Scene on the Eastern Railroad. — Action of the Legislature. — Colored Schools. — Controversy in Nantucket. — Petitions to the
Legislature. — Mr. Barrett's Bill. — Defeated. — Mr. Wilson's Motion to
reconsider. — Earnest Debate. — Reconsidered. — Bill passed. — Action
of Boston School Committee   .   .   .   .   488 - 498

CHAPTER XXXV.

POSITION OF THE COLORED PEOPLE. — FREDERICK DOUGLASS.

Sentiments of the Colored People. — Diverse Influences of Slavery and
Freedom. — Childhood of Frederick Douglass. — Cruelties of Slavery il-
lustrated. — Attempts to escape. — Sent to Baltimore. — Became a Ship-
caulker. — Escaped to New York. — Introduced to Mr. Ruggles. — Arrived
at New Bedford. — Works in a Ship-yard. — Addresses an Antislavery
Convention in Nantucket. — Impressions made upon Garrison and Rogers.
— Becomes Agent of the Massachusetts Antislavery Society. — Wonder-
ful Effects of his Speeches. — His Devotion to the Cause of his Race. —
Publishes his Autobiography. — Visits England. — Reasons for going. —
Establishes the "North Star." — Immense Labors of Twenty Years   499 - 511

CHAPTER XXXVI.

THE FLORIDA WAR. — SLAVERY ITS CAUSE.

The Surrender of Slaves by the Seminoles demanded. — The Additional
Treaty. — Agreement to remove to the West. — Outrages perpetrated by
Slave-traders. — Exasperation of the Indians. — Stern Policy of President
Jackson. — Seizure of Osceola's Wife. — Death of the Indian Agent. —
Destruction of Major Dade's Command. — Conduct of the Citizens of Flor-
ida. — Recall of General Scott. — Action of General Jessup. — Treaty of
Peace ; rejected by the Government. — The Slave-hunters. — Admissions
of General Jessup. — Bounty offered to the Creeks. — Dishonorable Con-
duct of Army Officers. — Honorable Action of the Cherokee Delegation.
— Cruel Action of the War Department. — Violation of Flags of Truce.
— Noble Conduct of General Taylor. — Treaty with the Creeks and Seminoles. — Danger of the Exiles. — Demands of the Creeks. — The Exiles
emigrate to Mexico. — The Faith and Honor of the Nation tarnished   512 - 527

CHAPTER XXXVII.

DEMAND FOR THE RECOGNITION OF PROPERTY IN SLAVES.

The Greed of Gain gratified by Slavery. — Mr. Whittlesey's Report. — Debates on the Question of Slave Property. — Spanish Treaty. — The Florida Claims. — Mr. Cooper's Report. — Mr. Giddings's and Mr. Adams's Speeches. — Payment for Slaves by the British Government. — Mr. Fillmore's Bill. — Speech of Mr. Giddings. — Violent Scenes in the House. — Degrading Influences of Slavery. — General Jessup's Contract with the Indians. — Watson's Claim. — General Gaines's Order. — His Honorable Conduct. — The Collins Claim. — Action of General Taylor. — Faithless Action of the Government. — Renewal of Watson's Claim. — Reports on the Claim. — Watson's Claim allowed. — Claim of Pacheco. — Failure of the Bill 528-544

CHAPTER XXXVIII.

THE LIBERTY PARTY.

Early Abolitionists pledged to Political Action. — Questioning Candidates. — Seward, Cushing, Fillmore, Brooks, Parmenter. — A Political Party demanded. — Myron Holley. — New York State Society calls a National Convention at Albany. — Opposed by the Board of Managers of the Massachusetts Society. — Meeting of the Convention. — Nomination of James G. Birney for President and Thomas Earle for Vice-President. — Small Vote. — Address of Committee. — Salmon P. Chase. — State Convention in Ohio. — Peterboro' Convention. — Address to the Slaves. — National Convention. — Resolutions. — Candidates. — Philadelphia Convention. — Professor Cleaveland's Address. — Election. — Western and Southwestern Convention. — Mr. Chase's Address. — Eastern Convention. — Dissensions. — Unconstitutionality of Slavery. — Divisions . . . 545-555

CHAPTER XXXIX.

MOBS. — ANTISLAVERY ACTIVITIES. — WOMEN'S FAIRS.

Riot at Cincinnati. — Cowardice of the City Government. — Manly Stand of Dr. Bailey. — Riot in Philadelphia. — Riots in New Bedford, Nantucket, and Portland. — Riotous Demonstrations in the North. — The Tone of the South. — Divisions among Abolitionists. — New Organization. — Old Organization. — Antislavery Fairs. — "Liberty Bell." — Address to the Slaves. — Address to President Tyler. — One hundred Conventions. — Thomas P. Beach. — Visit of Abolitionists to England. — Henry C. Wright. — Case of John L. Brown. — Decrease of Antislavery Societies. — Spread of Antislavery Sentiments. — The Impending Struggle . 556-567

CHAPTER XL.

NO UNION WITH SLAVEHOLDERS.

Meeting of the American Antislavery Society in 1842. — Debate on the
Issue of No Union with Slaveholders. — Meeting of the Massachusetts
Antislavery Society. — Protest against the Constitution by Mr. Foster. —
Mr. Garrison's Proposition. — Meeting of the American Antislavery So-
ciety in 1844. — The Doctrine of No Union with Slaveholders adopted.
— Protests. — Address to the Abolitionists. — Letter of Francis Jackson.
— Gerrit Smith's Letter to John G. Whittier. — Replies. — Disunion
Policy adopted   568–575

CHAPTER XLI.

IMPRISONMENT OF COLORED SEAMEN.

Imprisonment in South Carolina. — Laws of Louisiana. — Resolutions of
Massachusetts. — The Governor authorized to appoint Agents to defend
Colored Seamen. — Appointment of Mr. Hoar. — Excitement in South
Carolina. — Action of Governor Hammond. — Resolutions of South Caro- .
lina Legislature. — Fines and Imprisonments imposed upon Persons that
defend Negroes. — Indignation at Charleston. — Action of the Authori-
ties. — Mr. Hoar forced to leave the State. — Mr. Hubbard's Mission to
New Orleans. — Compelled to leave. — Petitions presented to Congress
by Mr. Winthrop. — Reports of Hoar and Hubbard. — Message of the
Governor. — Action of the Legislature   576–586

CHAPTER XLII.

PLOT FOR THE ANNEXATION OF TEXAS.

Dominating Influences of the Slave Power. — Texas. — Immigration from
the South. — Texas declared Independent. — Annexation to the United
States proposed. — Rejected by Mr. Van Buren. — Election and Death of
General Harrison. — Mr. Tyler. — Mr. Gilmer's Letter. — General Jackson's Letter. — Presidential Intrigue. — Address of Members of Congress
against the Texas Scheme. — Duff Green's Letter. — Visit of Mr. An-
drews and Mr. Tappan to England. — Motives for Annexation distinctly
avowed. — Accusations against England. — Position of the British Government. — Texas or Disunion. — Conditions demanded by Texas. —
Death of Mr. Upshur. — Mr. Calhoun made Secretary of State. —
Treaty   587–605

CHAPTER XLIII.

TEXAS PLOT CONSUMMATED.

Presidential Election. — The Issue distinctly presented. — Position of the
Whig and Democratic Parties. — Embarrassing Position of Antislavery
Men. — The Alabama Letter. — Secret Circular. — Mr. Walker's Letter.

— Election of Mr. Polk. — Meeting of Congress. — Mr. Benton's Bill. — Mr. Hale's Proposition. — Mr. Ingersoll's Resolution. — Mr. Hamlin's Motion. — The Debates. — Adoption of Mr. Brown's Amendment. — Passage of the Resolutions. — Reported against by the Senate Committee on Foreign Affairs. — Debates in the Senate. — Mr. Walker's Amendment. — Mr. Miller's Amendment. — Passage of Joint Resolutions. — Position of Southern Whigs. — Weakness or Treachery of Northern Democrats. — Action of Mr. Tyler. — Rejoicing of the Friends of Annexation 606 – 620

CHAPTER XLIV.

VERMONT AND MASSACHUSETTS. — JOHN P. HALE. — CASSIUS M. CLAY.

Action of Vermont and Massachusetts. — Massachusetts Anti-Texas Convention. — Proscriptive Policy of the New Administration. — John P. Hale. — Address to his Constituents. — Denounced by the Democrats of New Hampshire. — His Nomination withdrawn. — Appeal to the People. — " Independent Democrats." — The State canvassed by Mr. Hale. — Speeches of Hale and Pierce. — Coalition between the Whigs and Independent Democrats. — The Democracy defeated. — Mr. Hale elected United States Senator. — Brave Fight in the Senate. — Cassius M. Clay. — Opposes the Annexation of Texas. — Visits the Northern States. — Advocates the Election of Mr. Clay. — Returns to Kentucky. — Issues an Address to the People. — Establishes the " True American." — Boldly denounces Slaveholding. — Exasperation of Slaveholders. — They demand the Suppression of the Paper. — Refusal to comply with the Demand. — The Paper forcibly suppressed. — Mr. Clay appeals to the People. — Re-establishes his Paper . . . . 621 – 635

CHAPTER XLV.

TEXAS ADMITTED AS A SLAVE STATE.

Resolve of Antislavery Men to continue the Struggle. — Action of the Massachusetts Legislature. — Differences among leading Whigs. — Celebration of the 1st of August by the Abolitionists. — Anti-Texas Conventions held in Massachusetts. — Committee appointed. — Petitions against the Admission of Texas as a Slave State. — Meeting of Congress. — Presentation of Petitions. — Resolutions for the Admission as a State. — Speech of Mr. Rockwell. — Resolutions for Admission. — Considered in the Senate. — Protest of Mr. Webster. — Texas admitted. — Address of the Anti-Texas Committee. — Complete Victory of the Slave Power . . . 636 – 651

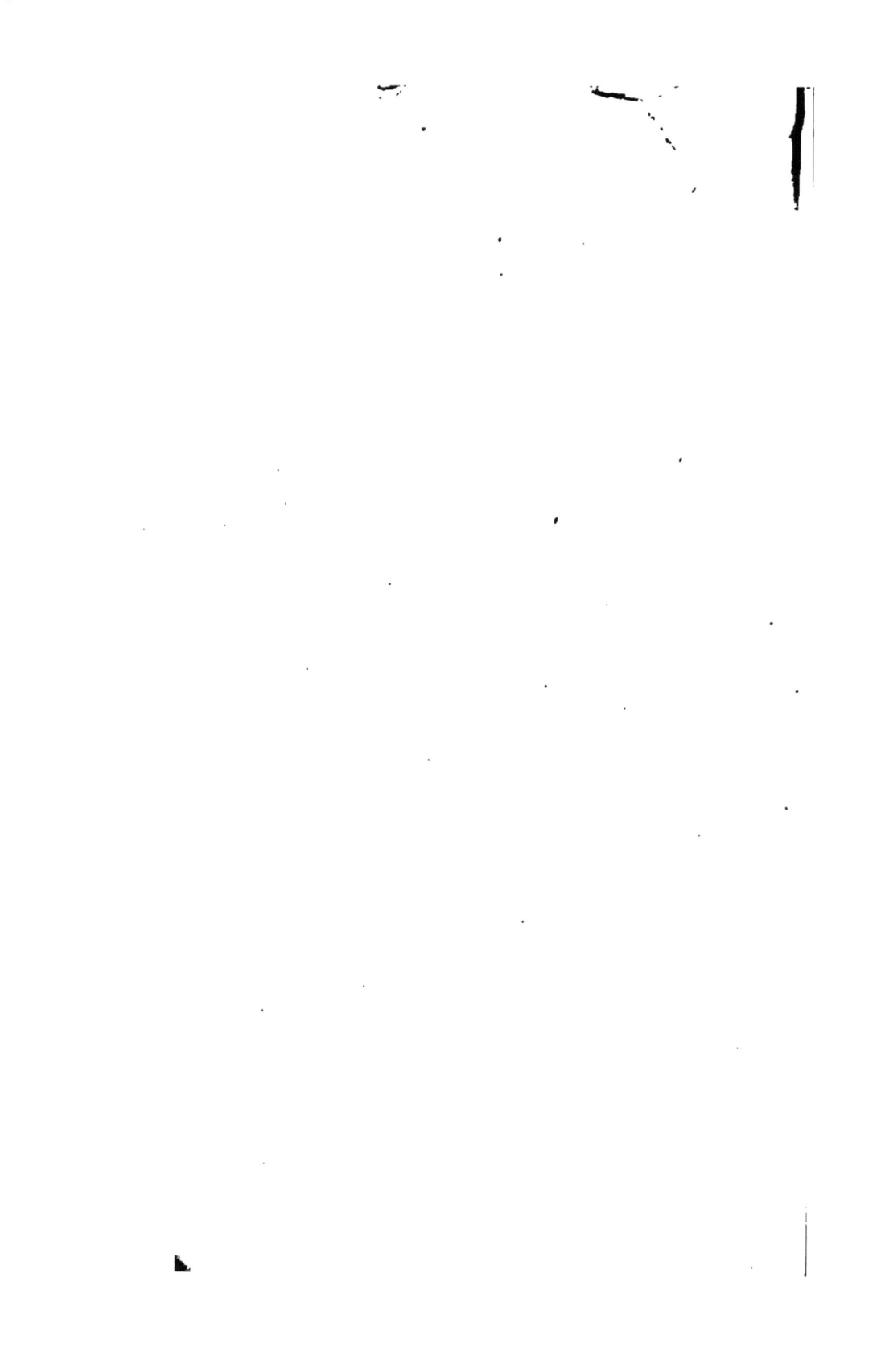

RISE AND FALL OF THE SLAVE POWER IN AMERICA.

CHAPTER I.

THE BEGINNINGS AND GROWTH OF SLAVERY AND THE EARLY DEVELOPMENT OF THE SLAVE POWER.

Basis of Slavery. — American Slavery. — Slave Power. — Issues of the Civil War. — African Slave-trade. — Slaves brought into Virginia. — Colonial and Commercial Policy of England. — Slave-trade encouraged. — Colonial Statutes annulled. — Spread of Slavery and Increase of Slave-trade. — Slavery in New England. — John Eliot. — Samuel Sewall. — Action of the Quakers. — Testimonies against Slavery by Burling, Sandiford, Lay, Woolman, Benezet, Wesley, Whitefield. — Emancipation advocated by Dr. Hopkins and Dr. Rush. — Opinions of the Revolutionary Leaders. — Slave-trade denounced by Congress. — South Carolina and Georgia for the Slave-trade. — Articles of Confederation. — Development of the Slave Power.

God's Holy Word declares that man was doomed to eat his bread in the sweat of his face. History and tradition teach that the indolent, the crafty, and the strong, unmindful of human rights, have ever sought to evade this Divine decree by filching their bread from the constrained and unpaid toil of others. From inborn indolence, conjoined with avarice, pride, and lust of power, has sprung slavery in all its Protean forms, from the mildest type of servitude to the harsh and hopeless condition of absolute and hereditary bondage. Thus have grown and flourished caste and privilege, those deadly foes of the rights and well-being of mankind, which can exist only by despoiling the many for the benefit of the few.

American slavery reduced man, created in the Divine image, to property. It converted a being endowed with conscience, reason, affections, sympathies, and hopes, into a chattel. It sunk a free moral agent, with rational attributes and immortal

1

aspirations, to merchandise. It made him a beast of burden in the field of toil, an outcast in social life, a cipher in the courts of law, and a pariah in the house of God. To claim himself, or to use himself for his own benefit or the benefit of wife or child, was deemed a crime. His master could dispose of his person at will, and of everything acquired by his enforced and unrequited toil.

This complete subversion of the natural rights of millions, by which they were " deemed, held, taken, reputed, and adjudged in law to be chattels personal to all intents, constructions, and purposes whatsoever," constituted a system antagonistic to the doctrines of reason and the monitions of conscience, and developed and gratified the most intense spirit of personal pride, a love of class distinctions, and the lust of dominion. Hence arose a commanding power, ever sensitive, jealous, proscriptive, dominating, and aggressive, which was recognized and fitly characterized as the Slave Power.

This slavery and this Slave Power, in their economical, social, moral, ecclesiastical, and political relations to the people and to the government, demoralizing the one and distracting the councils of the other, made up the vital issues of that " irrepressible conflict " which finally culminated in a civil war that startled the nations by its suddenness, fierceness, and gigantic proportions.

Half a century before the discovery of America, Portuguese and Spanish navigators had introduced African slaves into Europe. The English and other commercial nations followed their example. When, therefore, the Western Continent was opened to colonization and settlement, these nations were prepared to introduce slaves and to prosecute the African slave-traffic with vigor and on a large scale.

In the month of August, 1619, a Dutch ship entered James River with twenty African slaves. They were purchased by the colonists, and they and their offspring were held in perpetual servitude. Thus, at Jamestown, twelve years from the settlement of the colony of Virginia, and one year before the feet of the Pilgrims had touched the New World, began that system in the British continental colonies which, under the fostering care of England, overspread the land. So near in time, though remote in points of destination, came those two vessels across the sea, with elements at once so potent and yet so unlike,— the "Mayflower," with its freight of learning and Christian civilization ; the other, with its ill-starred burden of wretchedness and woe, bearing the seeds of a system destined, after a struggle of two hundred and forty years for development, expansion, and dominion, to light the fires of civil war, and perish in the flames its own hand had kindled.

During the years from 1619 to the opening of the American Revolution the friends of the slave-trade and of slavery controlled the government and dictated the policy of England. Her kings and queens, lords and commons, judges and attorney-generals, gave to the African slave-traffic their undeviating support. Her merchants and manufacturers clamored for its protection and extension. Her coffers were filled with gold bedewed with tears and stained with blood. "For more than a century," in the words of Horace Mann, "did the madness of this traffic rage. During all those years the clock of eternity never counted out a minute that did not witness the cruel death, by treachery or violence, of some father or mother of Africa."

Under the encouragement of British legislation and the fostering smile of royalty, more than three hundred thousand African bondmen were imported into the thirteen British colonies. The efforts of colonial legislation — whether dictated by humanity, interest, or fear — to check this traffic were defeated by the persistent policy of the British government. "Great Britain," in the words of Bancroft, "steadily rejecting every colonial restriction on the slave-trade, instructed the governors, on pain of removal, not to give even a temporary assent to such laws." The planters of Virginia, alarmed at the rapid increase of slaves, as early as 1726 imposed a tax to check their importation, but "the interfering interest of the African company obtained the repeal of that law." South Carolina attempted restrictions upon the importation of slaves as late as 1760, for which she received the rebuke of the British authorities. The legislature of Pennsylvania, as early as 1712, passed an act to prevent the increase of slaves; but that act was annulled by the Crown. The legislature of Massachusetts, in 1771, and again in 1774, adopted measures for the abolition of the slave-trade; but they failed to receive the approval of the colonial governors. Queen Anne, who had reserved for herself one quarter of the stock of the Royal African Company, that gigantic monopolist of the slave-trade, charged it to furnish full supplies of slaves to the colonies of New York and New Jersey, and instructed the governors of those colonies to give due encouragement to that company; and it was the testimony of Madison that the British government constantly checked the attempts of his native State " to put a stop to this infernal traffic." Up to the hour of American Independence, the government of England steadily resisted colonial restrictions on the slave-trade, and persisted in forcing this traffic, so gainful to her commercial and manufacturing interests, upon her colonies, " which," in the words of the Earl of Dartmouth, ir 1775, " were not allowed to check or discourage in any degree a traffic so beneficial to the nation." British avarice planted slavery in America; British legislation sanctioned and maintained it; British statesmen sustained and guarded it.

But the British government and British merchants were not alone responsible for the spread of slavery in the colonies. The inhabitants themselves were generally only too willing to profit by such enforced and unpaid toil. North Carolina was settled by colonies from Virginia, who carried slaves with them. Governor Sir John Yeamans brought slaves with him from Barbadoes into South Carolina, and planted slavery there. Georgia, however, was settled by colonies under the lead of James Oglethorpe, who held slavery to be a horrid crime against the gospel, as well as against the laws of England, and slavery was there forbidden. Some of the colonists, however, soon began to complain that they were prohibited the use of slave-labor. The laws were evaded; slaves from South Carolina were hired, at first for short periods, and afterwards for life. Soon slave-ships sailed from Savannah for the coast of Africa, and slaves were introduced with the connivance of the British government, and Georgia became a slave State. Slavery also readily found its way into the colonies of Maryland, Delaware, and Pennsylvania. The company interested in the colonization of New Jersey offered a land bounty of seventy-five acres for every slave introduced there. And the Royal African Company was enjoined by Queen Anne "to have a constant and sufficient supply of merchantable negroes" for this colony. The Dutch West India Company promised to supply the Dutch settlers of New York with slaves, — a promise afterwards renewed. They were then allowed to purchase slaves of others, and finally to engage in the foreign traffic itself. Nor did the rugged soil, or the still more rugged clime, of New England save its colonies from the introduction of the system even there. Slavery, however, grew slowly. In 1680 it was stated by Governor Bradstreet that there were only about one hundred and twenty African slaves in the colony of Massachusetts. At the end of a hundred years from the settlement of Plymouth there were estimated to be only about two thousand.

During the half-century preceding the Revolution slavery increased with rapidity, especially in the Southern colonies. There the production of tobacco, indigo, and rice became of great commercial importance to the mother country, and slavery felt its stimulating influence. There slaves toiled generally on large plantations, often under merciless overseers and the menace of the lash. In the colonies north of Mason and Dixon's line they were either employed in the families of the wealthy or belonged to small farmers who labored with their own servants and usually received them into their families. From this circumstance, and from the fact that they were accorded privileges under the laws and in the usages and customs of society, their condition was rendered more tolerable, and their character was less degraded than were the character and condition of Southern slaves.

In spite, however, of the avarice which guided and inspired the commercial and colonial policy of England, in spite of the corrupting influence of the slave-trade and of slavery itself, they found sturdy opposers in both England and America. The colonial legislature of Massachusetts of 1641 enacted in its code, styled the "Body of Liberties," that there should never be any bond-slavery, unless it be of captives taken in "just war," or of such as willingly sold themselves or were sold to them, and such should have the liberties and Christian usages that God had established in Israel. Whether this act prohibited the slavery of Africans or not has been a question freely discussed, and on which differences of opinion have obtained. There can be no doubt, however, that the colonists of that day made a distinction between slaves captured in "just war" and those stolen in Africa, and that this act was based on this distinction. At any rate, it is safe to say that the servitude it authorized, with its recognized limitations of the Mosaic code, had little in common with the American slavery which afterwards obtained in all the colonies.

In 1646 two slaves were introduced into the colony by a member of a church, who had procured them in a slave-hunt in Africa. A memorial immediately presented to the General Court, setting forth the threefold outrage of " murder, man-stealing, and Sabbath-breaking," — the slave-hunt having taken place on the Sabbath, — drew forth a stringent order. " Conceiving themselves," they said, " bound by the first opportunity to bear witness against the heinous and crying sin of man-stealing," they supplemented their testimony with the requirement that the victims " should be sent to their native country, Guinea, and a letter," expressing " the indignation of the court thereabout." In November of that year it was enacted that " if any man stealeth a man, or mankind, he shall surely be put to death." The colony of Connecticut, in 1650, and the colony of New Haven, soon after, passed acts making man-stealing a capital offence.

Whatever differences of opinion there may have been concerning the full import and effects of the Massachusetts act of 1641, there can be none concerning that of the colony of Rhode Island, adopted in 1652. By this act it was provided that no " black mankind or white," " being forced by covenant-bond or otherwise," should serve more than ten years, or after the age of twenty-four years, but should be set free. " This noble act," says Moore, in his " Notes on Slavery in Massachusetts," "stands out in solitary grandeur in the middle of the seventeenth century, the first legislative enactment in the history of this continent, if not of the world, for the suppression of involuntary servitude." It was in view of this early legislation against African slavery and the slave-trade, and of the small number of slaves that found their way into the Massachusetts colonies during the first two generations of their history, that Whittier says: "It was not the rigor of her northern winter, nor the unfriendly soil of Massachusetts, which discouraged the introduction of slavery during the first half of the century of her existence as a colony. It was the recognition of the brotherhood of man in sin, suffering, and redemption, the awful responsibilities and eternal destinies of humanity, her hatred of wrong and tyranny, and her stern sense of justice, which led her to impose upon the African slave-trade the terrible penalty of the Mosaic code."

In spite, however, of this early legislation, and of the popular sentiment which prompted it, slavery made progress, the number of slaves slowly increased, and men were found ready to engage in the infamous traffic. The demoralizing influence of the Indian wars, and the recognition of the principle that captives taken in them might be rightfully held in bondage, contributed largely to this result. There were, however, earnest and faithful protestants who saw and deeply deplored the great and grievous wrong thus inflicted on both the Indian and the African. John Eliot, the apostle to the Indians, presented, in 1675, a memorial to the Governor and Council against selling captured Indians into slavery. His objections were that it prolonged the war, that it hindered the enlargement of Christ's kingdom, and that "the selling of souls is a dangerous merchandise." Though the mission of this large-hearted man was mainly with the Indians, he did not forget the African, but lamented, it is said by Cotton Mather, with "a bleeding and burning passion," "the destroying ignorance" in which they were left, by men bearing the name of Christian, "for fear of losing the benefit of their vassalage."

The iniquity of slavery and of the slave-trade, and the wrongs of the slave, were deeply felt by Justice Samuel Sewall, afterwards Chief Justice of the Supreme Court of Massachusetts. In the year 1700 he wrote a pamphlet entitled "The Selling of Joseph: A Memorial," in which slavery was characterized, and the primal truths of human equality and obligation were enunciated, with signal boldness and force. He maintained that "originally and naturally" there was no such thing as slavery; and that "these Ethiopians, as black as they are, seeing they are the sons and daughters of the first Adam, the brethren and sisters of the last Adam, and the offspring of God, they ought to be treated with respect agreeable."

Although this production was received, its faithful and fearless author says, "with frowns and hard words," there was a state of unrest in the public mind which revealed itself in various ways. The slaves themselves were uneasy under their bondage, and made no secret of their earnest longings for liberty. Though their increase was small, the most thoughtful and conscientious viewed that increase with apprehension, and earnestly desired the abolition of both the trade and the system. During the ten years immediately preceding the Declaration of Independence, in which the rights of man and of the colonies were under sharp discussion, the wrongfulness and inconsistency of slavery became more and more apparent. The desire for emancipation and the extinction of the slave-trade found utterance in sermons and pamphlets, some thorough and of decided merit, and in the resolutions and memorials of towns praying the legislature to take action at once in the interests of humanity and true patriotism.

But members of the society of Friends took the lead in this opposition. In the year 1688 a small body of German Quakers, at Germantown, Pennsylvania, presented a protest to the Yearly Meeting against the "buying, selling, and holding men in slavery." But though not then prepared to take action, it sent forth in 1696 the advice that "the members should discourage the introduction of slavery, and be careful of the moral and intellectual training of such as they held in servitude." Three years before this advice was given, George Keith, then a member of that society, had denounced slavery as contrary to the religion of Christ, the rights of man, and sound reason and policy, and charged its members to "set their negroes at liberty after some reasonable time of service."

In New England the Quakers, at the Monthly Meeting at Dartmouth in 1716, sent to the Rhode Island Quarterly Meeting the query, "whether it be agreeable to truth for the Friends to purchase slaves and keep them for a term of life." The Quakers of Nantucket in the same year, moved by the eloquence of the wife of Nathaniel Starbuck, a preacher of their denomination, sent forth the declaration that "it is not agreeable to the truth for Friends to purchase slaves and hold them for the term of life." In 1729 they made an earnest appeal to the Philadelphia Yearly Meeting, in which they say : "Inasmuch as we are restrained by the rule of discipline from being concerned in fetching or importing negro slaves from their own country, whether it is not as reasonable that we should be restricted from buying them when imported." At that time Elihu Coleman wrote a pamphlet against making men slaves, because it was "anti-christian" and "very opposite both to grace and nature."

Most faithful testimony against slavery was borne by William Burling, of Long Island, in the Yearly Meeting of the Friends. In 1729 Ralph Sandiford published "The Mystery of Iniquity," in which he earnestly condemned the sin of oppression. The ardent but eccentric Benjamin Lay, who had witnessed in Barbadoes scenes of cruelty to slaves that disturbed and distressed his sensitive nature, pleaded the cause of the bondman in a volume, published in 1737 by Benjamin Franklin. From 1746 to 1767 John Woolman, of New Jersey, travelled much in the Middle and Southern colonies, proclaiming to Christians that "the practice of continuing slavery is not right," and that "liberty is the natural right of all men equally." This humane, unselfish, and self-denying man, as he travelled among the people, saw "a dark gloominess overhanging the land," and "a spirit of fierceness and love of dominion." But, notwithstanding all that was calculated to depress and sadden his heart, he labored on with earnest and unconquerable zeal, and largely contributed to the work of preparing his denomination

2

to bear their early testimony against the sin and practice of slavery.

But the most active antislavery worker of that age was Anthony Benezet, the son of Huguenot parents, who escaped from France on account of the revocation of the Edict of Nantes. Having inherited an intense and passionate love of liberty, and becoming deeply affected by the iniquity of the slave-trade and the cruelty exercised toward slaves by their owners, he earnestly lifted up his voice on behalf of the oppressed, and strove to awaken Christians to a just sense of the sin of slaveholding. He established and taught gratuitously an evening school for the instruction of negroes. Under his pious labors their moral and religious advancement recommended the colored race to the notice of influential persons, too much accustomed to hold it in contempt. Among his many publications was an historical account of Guinea, which is said to have given an impulse to the mind of Thomas Clarkson, who afterward labored so effectively for the abolition of the slave-trade by the British government. He exerted himself to induce the legislature of Pennsylvania, in 1780, to begin the work of emancipation.

By the faithful and self-denying labors of these devoted pioneers and early advocates of antislavery, and others of less note, covering a period of a hundred years, was the society of Friends at length persuaded to rid itself of the system of enforced servitude. Nor was this great work accomplished without much of exciting discussion, stern rebuke, and stirring appeal. For with them, as with others, the love of ease and the lust of dominion were strong, nor did they at once and easily let go their hold on the victims of their power. And not until the conscience of the society was aroused by the unequivocal decisions of its ecclesiastical tribunals, showing slavery to be a sin to be repented of and forsaken, did it achieve the high distinction of being the first and only denomination to purge itself entirely of this great iniquity.

Nor were the people without remonstrance and warning from strangers, who, seeing the abomination of the system, boldly denounced its essential cruelty and wickedness. John Wesley, who visited the country during the early part of the last century, unequivocally condemned it. His terse and trenchant characterization of slavery, so often repeated, — that it was " the sum of all villanies," — was only one of many sharp things he uttered. He called the system " the vilest that ever saw the sun," and denominated " slave-dealers man-stealers, — the worst of thieves, in comparison with whom highway robbers and housebreakers are comparatively innocent." To these emphatic words he added that " men-buyers are exactly on a level with men-stealers."

In 1739 George Whitefield, the renowned pulpit-orator and evangelist, having travelled extensively through the Southern States, addressed to their inhabitants a " Letter," in which he combined the impressions of an eyewitness with the reflections of a Christian teacher. Affirming that his sympathies had been strongly excited by the " miseries of the poor negroes," he called attention to the practice of slave-masters, and the encouragement it afforded to the savage tribes in Africa to continue their warfare on each other, to supply the demand for slaves thus created. He charged the " generality of " them with using their slaves " as bad as though they were brutes ; nay, worse," — worse than their horses, which were " fed and properly cared for " after the labors of the day, while the slaves must grind their corn and prepare their own food, — worse even than their dogs, who are " caressed and fondled," while the slaves " are scarce permitted to pick up the crumbs which fall from their master's table." He spoke of the cruel lashings which "ploughed their backs and made long furrows," sometimes ending in death. He reminded them of their spacious houses and sumptuous fare ; while they to whose " indefatigable labors " their luxuries were " owing " had neither convenient food to eat nor proper raiment to put on.

Among the earlier apostles of emancipation was Dr. Samuel Hopkins, pastor of the Congregational Church in Newport, Rhode Island, who was as much distinguished for his advocacy of the doctrines of human rights as of the doctrines of the school of theology which bears his name. In 1770 he deliberately and solemnly resolved to attack the system of kidnapping, purchasing, and retaining slaves. Although Rhode Island had, as early as 1652, passed an act against the purchase of negroes, she had become deeply involved in the slave-trade. Newport was the great slave-mart of New England. Cargoes of slaves were often landed near the church and home of the great divine. Before his congregation, thus deeply involved in the guilt of slave-trading and slaveholding, he boldly rebuked the sin and pleaded the cause of its victims in a discourse of great plainness and power. It was an unselfish and heroic act, imperilling his position both as a pastor and as a recognized leader in the church. Of this noble act Whittier says: " It may well be doubted whether, on that Sabbath day, the angels of God, in their wide survey of His universe, looked upon a nobler spectacle than that of the minister of Newport, rising up before his slaveholding congregation, and demanding, in the name of the Highest, ' the deliverance of the captive and the opening of prison doors to them that were bound ! ' "

From 1770 to 1776 Dr. Hopkins repeatedly spoke on behalf of the slave, visited from house to house, and urged masters to free their bondmen. In the latter year he published his dialogue concerning slavery, together with his address to slaveholders. He dedicated this remarkable production, said to have been " the ablest document which had at that time and on that theme appeared in the English language," to the Continental Congress. It had a large circulation among the statesmen of that day, and exerted a potent influence on public opinion. This early champion of the black man was cheered by the passage, in 1774, of a law prohibiting the importation of negroes into Rhode Island ; and, in 1784, by the passage of an act declaring all children born after the next March free, — results to which he had largely contributed by his early, persistent, and self-denying labors. His heart was gladdened, too, by the action of his church. Instructed by his teachings and inspired by his zeal, it declared slavery to be " a gross violation of the righteousness and benevolence of the gospel," and therefore it resolved, " We will not tolerate it in this church."

In 1773 Dr. Benjamin Rush, an eminent physician, philanthropist, and statesman, published in Philadelphia " An Address to the Inhabitants of the British Settlements in America on Slave-keeping." In this address he combated the idea so persistently pressed by the supporters of the slave-trade, that it was impossible to carry on the production of sugar, rice, and indigo without negro slaves. " No manufactory," he said, with refreshing boldness and fidelity to truth, " can ever be of consequence enough to society to admit the least violation of the laws of justice or humanity." This early abolitionist eloquently pleaded the cause of " the unhappy Africans transported to America." Of the slave-traffic he said: " Future ages, when they read the accounts of the slave-trade, if they do not regard them as fabulous, will be at a loss which to condemn most, our folly or our guilt in abetting this direct violation of nature and religion."

These utterances of those earlier apostles of emancipation awoke responses in the bosoms of many of their countrymen. During the years of agitation preceding the Revolution, in which the liberties of the colonies and the rights of man were discussed with masterly power by the most gifted minds of the country, many of the popular leaders of New England, the Middle colonies, and even of Virginia, did not fail to see and to acknowledge the wrongfulness of slavery, and to denounce the slave-traffic and the slave-extending policy of the British government. Many slave-masters, who afterward aided in inaugurating the Revolution, in fighting its battles, and carrying the country over from colonial dependence to national independence, were hostile not only to the slave-trade, but to the existence of slavery itself.

On the 20th of October, 1774, the first Continental Congress signed and promulgated the Articles of Association. In that bond of union, which laid the foundation of the new nation, the pledge was made that the United Colonies would "neither import nor purchase any slave," and would " wholly discontinue the slave-trade." The explicit declaration was added, that any persons violating these Articles of Association should be pronounced " foes to the rights of British America," " universally contemned as the foes of American liberty," " unworthy

of the rights of freemen." This union of the inhabitants' of
the thirteen British colonies, thus making one people, was
begun with a solemn pledge wholly to abstain from all par-
ticipation in a traffic then supported by the commercial nations of Europe. The Articles of Association, containing these
explicit pledges, were adopted by colonial conventions, county
meetings, and lesser assemblages throughout the country, and
became the fundamental Constitution of the first American
Union.

That Congress gave expression to the general sentiment of
the people of the colonies fully appears in the declarations of
the North Carolina and Virginia conventions, which sent delegates to that Congress. These conventions pledged themselves
not to import slaves, and not to purchase them when imported
by others. In Georgia — a colony founded by James Oglethorpe, who forbade slavery there, but whose humane purposes
were afterward thwarted by avarice and power — a public
meeting declared " their disapprobation and abhorrence of the
unnatural practice of slavery in America," and pledged their
" utmost endeavors for the manumission of slaves in our colony." And Congress itself, on the 6th of April, 1776, resolved,
without opposition, that " no slave be imported into any of the
thirteen united colonies."

The British commercial and colonial policy, however, had
interested, active, and influential supporters. Leading statesmen in South Carolina and Georgia were confessedly not only
for slavery, but for the continuance of the slave-trade. In
Maryland, Virginia, and North Carolina slavery had still a
strong hold upon the people. But their interest in the domestic quickened their opposition to the foreign slave-traffic.
Although there were but few negroes in the Middle and New-
England colonies, many of these having been made free by the
voluntary action of their masters, still slavery and the slave-
trade had zealous supporters, especially among the commercial,
wealthy, and aristocratic classes. This fact was signally manifested by the action of Congress in striking from the original
draft of the Declaration of Independence Mr. Jefferson's arraignment of the British king for forcing upon his American

colonies that traffic in men which he branded as an "execrable commerce," "a piratical warfare," "the opprobrium of infidel powers," "a cruel war against human nature." "That clause reprobating the enslaving of the inhabitants of Africa was struck out," its illustrious author declares, "in complaisance to South Carolina and Georgia, who had never attempted to restrain the importation of slaves, and who, on the contrary, still wished to continue it. Our Northern brethren, also, I believe, felt a little tender under those censures. Although their people had very few slaves themselves, yet they had been pretty considerable carriers of them to others."

The same spirit and policy which struck these words from the Declaration of Independence influenced the action of Congress in framing the Articles of Confederation. The report of the committee to prepare a plan provided that supplies should be obtained by requisitions on each State in proportion to the number of its inhabitants. This at once and necessarily raised the question of the *status* of the slave. Mr. Chase, of Maryland, afterwards one of the justices of the Supreme Court of the United States, moved to count only the white inhabitants. "The negroes," he said, "were property, and no more members of the state than cattle."

It was suggested by Mr. Harrison, of Virginia, that two slaves should be counted as one freeman. Mr. Wilson, of Pennsylvania, said the exemption of slaves from taxation would be "the greatest encouragement to slave-keeping and the importation of slaves." He declared that they increased products and imposed burdens, and prevented freemen from cultivating the country. "Dismiss your slaves," he said; "freemen will take their places."

To this remark Mr. Lynch, of South Carolina, replied with emphasis, "Our slaves are our property; if that is debated, there is an end of confederation." He asked why they should "be taxed more than sheep." To this question Franklin replied: "Sheep will never make insurrections." Mr. Chase's amendment was rejected. Georgia was divided, and all the States north of Mason and Dixon's line voted against it.

The obstacles in the way of Confederation being found so

great, the discussion was then suspended; but it was resumed again in October, 1777. It was then moved that the supplies be based on the value of property in each State. This proposition was rejected, and a motion was made to exempt slaves from taxation. The four New England States voted against it, New York and Pennsylvania were divided, and Maryland, Virginia, North Carolina, South Carolina, and New Jersey voted for it. This vote exempted slaves from taxation altogether, either as inhabitants or property. It was a complete triumph of those representing the slave interest, and may be counted among the earlier illustrations of the potent influence of the rising Slave Power.

No power was given to the Confederation to regulate commerce. Each State was left free to decide what imports it would admit or prohibit, so that Congress, after its emphatic condemnation by the acts of 1774 and 1776, " renounced forever," in the words of Bancroft, " the power to sanction or to stop the slave-trade." This result could not but enure to the interests of slavery and to the strengthening of its power.

But the Confederation secured to the free inhabitants of the State all privileges and immunities of the citizens of the several States. The legislature of South Carolina, when the Articles of Confederation were under consideration, saw that by this provision the rights of inter-citizenship were secured to the free colored inhabitants of all the States. After debate, the plan of Confederation was returned to Congress with the recommendation that inter-citizenship should be confined to white persons. South Carolina and Georgia supported the proposed change, but eight States refusing their assent, the proposition was lost. In this instance freedom won, and the claims of human equality were vindicated.

But it cannot be doubted that at the time of the Declaration of Independence, when the government of England ended and the government of the United States began, the people were, on the grounds of justice, humanity, and interest, largely in favor of putting an end to the African slave-trade. Neither can it be doubted that the most conscientious and enlightened portion of the people, including most of the Revo-

lutionary leaders, who guided the colonies through civil war
to national unity and independence, believed slavery to be inconsistent with the doctrines they were proclaiming and the
civil institutions they were founding.   The statesmen of that
era hoped, and confidently expected, that it would soon pass ·
away.   But the slave system, fostered by England and sustained by individual interest, indolence, and pride, during a
hundred and fifty years, had so incorporated · itself into the
social life of the people, especially of the South, that, when
menaced by the logic of events, it was seen to have a hold and
tenacity of life not dreamed of by either friend or foe.   Champions were ready not only to protect it against the advancing
currents of Christian civilization, but also to oppose every
·interest, every institution, and every individual that menaced
its paramount sway.   Even then, when the Republic took its
place in the family of nations, had begun and had far advanced
that work of personal and public deterioration, — that poison-
ing of the fountains of individual and social life whose full
development the Rebellion revealed, as it was itself their sad
and legitimate result.

CHAPTER II.

ABOLITION. — ABOLITION SOCIETIES.

Articles of Association of the Colonies. — Colored Soldiers. — Slavery abolished in Massachusetts and Pennsylvania. — The Pennsylvania Abolition Society. — New York Abolition Society. — Rhode Island Abolition Society. — The Abolition Societies of Connecticut, New Jersey, Maryland, and Virginia. — Character of the Members of the Abolition Societies. — National Conventions.

THE Republic of the United States commenced its independent existence by the proclamation of the self-evident truths that all men are created equal, that all have an inalienable right to liberty, and that governments are instituted to secure these rights. Thus, in the Articles of Association and in the Declaration of Independence, pronounced by John Hancock " the ground and foundation of future government," these fundamental doctrines were recognized : that all men are by nature free, and that the American government was founded on the rights of human nature. Nor was this comprehensive assertion of rights limited by race or color. " The new republic," in the words of Bancroft, " as it took its place among the powers of the world, proclaimed its faith in the truth, reality, and unchangeableness of freedom, virtue, and right." This "assertion of right was made for the entire world of mankind and all coming generations, without any exception whatever."

When the United States joined the family of nations there were in the country about half a million persons of African descent. Nearly all were slaves; although there were a few, especially in the Eastern States, who had been emancipated. Some of these bore an honorable part in the War of Independence. Crispus Attucks, a colored patriot, was a leader, and the first martyr in the Boston massacre, on the 5th of March, 1770, which so fired the hearts and aroused the patriotism of the people. One of that race mingled his blood with the fallen patriots of the 19th of April, 1775. The sons of Africa fought side by side with their countrymen of the white race at Bunker Hill, where Major Pitcairn, as he stormed the works, fell mortally wounded by the shot of Salem, a black soldier. Indeed, it is hardly too much to say that some of the most heroic deeds of the War of Independence were performed by black men.

Rhode Island raised a colored regiment, commanded by Colonel Christopher Greene, the hero of Red Bank. Of the men of this regiment Governor Eustis, of Massachusetts, who had been Secretary of War under Jefferson, said in Congress, in 1820: "They discharged their duty with zeal and fidelity. The gallant defence of Red Bank, in which this regiment bore a part, is among the proofs of their valor." Tristam Burgess also said, in the House of Representatives, in 1828, that "no braver men met the enemy in battle." Of the conduct of these men in the Battle of Rhode Island, — pronounced by Lafayette "the best fought battle of the war," — Arnold, in his "History of Rhode Island," says: "It was in repelling these furious onsets that the newly raised black regiment, under Colonel Greene, distinguished itself by deeds of desperate valor. Posted behind a thicket in the valley, they three times drove back the Hessians, who charged repeatedly down the hill to dislodge them."

Connecticut raised a battalion of black soldiers, and Colonel David Humphrey, attached to the military family of Washington, accepted a command in this corps. The heroic defence of Fort Griswold, on the heights of Groton, by Colonel Ledyard and his brave comrades, was among the most brilliant achievements of the war. When the works were stormed, the British officer, exasperated by the heroic resistance encountered, inquired, "Who commands this fort?" "I did; you do now," replied Ledyard, handing the officer his sword, which was instantly seized and run through his own body. Lambert, a negro soldier, avenged the murder of his commander by thrusting his bayonet through the British officer, and then fell himself, pierced with thirty-three bayonet wounds.

The right of free negroes to bear arms in the country's defence was not disputed in the more Northern colonies. At the opening of the war the Committee of Safety, in Massachusetts, declared that no slave should be admitted into the army upon any consideration whatever, as it would be " inconsistent with the principles that are to be supported, and reflect dishonor on this colony." Many were emancipated on condition of entering the army. Not always, however, did they receive the reward due to their bravery. In Maryland and Virginia, some who had served with fidelity to the close of the war were afterward dishonorably and wickedly reduced to slavery. When the heel of British tyranny was resting heavily on South Carolina and Georgia, Colonel John Laurens, a member of Washington's military family, sought to fill the patriot ranks by emancipating slaves and enrolling them in the ranks of the country's defenders. This eminently wise and patriotic effort, though encouraged by Congress, and sanctioned by Washington, met with little success ; and that heroic son of South Carolina, whose life, near the close of hostilities, was given to the country, was forced to declare that " avarice, pusillanimity, and prejudice " defeated the measure.

In the midst of the war all the States, with the exception of Connecticut and Rhode Island, framed and adopted constitutions. The settlers of Vermont, in 1777, framed a constitution forever excluding slavery from that Commonwealth ; but it did not become a State until after the adoption of the Federal Constitution. The constitution of Massachusetts was adopted in 1780. Its Bill of Rights declares that " all men are born free and equal, and have certain natural, essential, and inalienable rights ; among which may be reckoned the right of enjoying and defending their lives and liberties."

Before the adoption of this constitution several unsuccessful attempts had been made to extirpate slavery and the slave traffic. A bill for that purpose had been introduced in 1767 ; and three measures for the prohibition of the slave-trade had failed to receive executive approval. After the commencement of the war petitions were presented to the legislature in favor of emancipation. Among these petitions was one presented in 1777 by several colored persons, praying that they might

" be restored to the enjoyment of that freedom which is the natural right of all men." It was referred to a committee, which promptly reported a bill " to prevent the practice of holding persons in slavery." It declared that " the practice of holding Africans, and the children born of them, or any other person in slavery is unjustifiable in a civil government at a time when they are asserting their natural rights to freedom." Before acting upon this bill, the legislature, fearing to give offence to some of the States, addressed a letter to the Continental Congress to ascertain its views concerning the expediency of such action. In this letter they say : " Convinced of the justice of the measure, we are restrained from passing it only from an apprehension that our brethren in the other colonies should conceive there was an impropriety in our determining on a question which may in its nature and operation be of extensive influence, without previously consulting your Honors." " And," they continue, " we ask the attention of your Honors to this matter, that, if consistent with the union and harmony of the United States, we may follow the dictates of our own understanding and feelings ; at the same time assuring your Honors that we have such a sacred regard to the union and harmony of the United States as to conceive ourselves under obligation to refrain from any measure that should have a tendency to injure that union which is the basis of our defence and happiness." To this communication, breathing the spirit of freedom, the desire to do justly, and their intense anxiety to preserve harmony, and not to break with the other States, no response was returned.

What, however, Massachusetts failed to effect by direct legislation was secured indirectly through the decisions of her Supreme Court based on a clause in her Bill of Rights. Cases soon arose involving the question of the legality of slavery under her new constitution in which such eminent lawyers and statesmen as Levi Lincoln, Caleb Strong, and Theodore Sedgwick were engaged in behalf of those claiming their freedom. By one of these decisions a master had lost ten slaves. In a memorial to the legislature for relief he urged as a reason for his plea that " by the determination of the Supreme Court the said

clause in the Bill of Rights is so to be construed as to operate
to the total discharge and manumission of all negro servants
whatsoever." So Massachusetts, while yet the war was raging
for national independence, and before that independence was
recognized by the treaty of peace, became a free State ; taking
her place in the van, — a relative position she has honorably
maintained, not indeed without some faltering and mistakes,
in the long struggle with slavery and the Slave Power.

In 1780 Pennsylvania, under the lead of George Bryan, and,
no doubt, largely influenced by the indefatigable Anthony Benezet, who is said to have had a personal conference with every
member of her legislature, passed "an act of gradual abolition,"
by which the importation of slaves was prohibited, and all persons born or brought into the State were made free. The minority, however, entered their protest; " because," they say, " if the
time ever comes when slaves might be safely emancipated, we
cannot agree to their being made free citizens in so extensive
a manner." These protesting legislators further expressed
their belief that the negroes would be satisfied " without giving them the right of voting for and being voted into office."
In 1784 New Hampshire, like Massachusetts, became a free
State by the judicial interpretation of her constitution.

The Virginia Assembly, on motion of Jefferson, in 1778,
prohibited the further introduction of slaves; and in 1782 the
old colonial statute was repealed, which forbade emancipations
except for meritorious services. During this repeal, which
continued in force for ten years, a large number of such manu-
missions took place. It was, however, subsequently re-enacted ;
and that source of just and humane individual action, being
forcibly stopped, gradually dried up and ceased to flow. Maryland, like Virginia, both prohibited the introduction of slaves
and removed the restriction on individual emancipation.

In the same year, immediately after the close of the war, the
Pennsylvania Abolition Society was resuscitated. It had been
organized before the Revolution, being the first abolition society ever formed, as it is now the oldest in the world. Its
primary purpose was indicated by its name, "The society for
the relief of free negroes, unlawfully held in bondage." In its

preamble it was stated that many were unlawfully held in bondage who were "justly entitled to their freedom by the laws and constitution." John Baldwin was its first president. A Committee of Inspection was appointed, whose title, in connection with the name of the society, sufficiently indicates the functions of their office. During the first year of its existence it was eminently successful in its operations. But the breaking out and progress of the war diverted and absorbed public attention. The active prosecution of its chosen work was mostly suspended, and no meetings were held until the year 1784. Although there are no records of its doings, it is not probable that such men were idle during that eventful period.

Upon its resuscitation the society commenced operations with great vigor, extending them wherever there were evils, incident to slavery, to be remedied or removed. As it became known and appreciated, men eminent for public service became members. In 1787 it revised its constitution, enlarged both its name and range of effort, and became "The Pennsylvania Society for promoting the abolition of slavery, the relief of free negroes unlawfully held in bondage, and for improving the condition of the African race." The illustrious Franklin was made its president. By accepting this trust and actively discharging its duties, he not only honored himself and the society, but he did much to vindicate his great reputation. By it he showed that among the statesmen of his day he was unseduced by sophistries and compromises, and remained true to the doctrine of human rights and the self-evident truths of the Declaration of Independence. It showed him, too, as distinguished for his broad philanthropy as for his practical sagacity; indeed, that his philanthropy was the highest style and development of that sagacity.

Thus reorganized and officered, it entered vigorously upon its long and honorable mission. Among its first acts was the distribution of copies of its constitution and the act for the gradual abolition of slavery in Pennsylvania to the governors of the several States. It also opened a correspondence with eminent men in the United States, England, and France. It

was a live society, catholic in its membership, and national and
world-wide in the reach and range of its purposes and plans.
Thus, learning that vessels were still surreptitiously fitted out
in Pennsylvania for the slave-trade, it petitioned the legislature
for a supplementary law to prevent it; and the law was enacted.   Hearing that slave-ships were fitted out in Rhode
Island for a similar purpose, it at once called the attention of
the citizens of that State to the disgraceful traffic.   In 1790 it
addressed a memorial to Congress, signed by its distinguished
president, asking that body to " step to the very verge of its
power " in behalf of those held in bondage.   Year after year,
for almost half a century, it continued to memorialize Congress
against oppression, and in the interests of humanity and freedom.   It brought a case before the Supreme Court of Pennsylvania involving the question "whether slavery in any modi-
fication whatever is not inconsistent with the constitution of
the State."   Though the decision of the court was adverse, this
effort revealed its activity and fidelity.

Ever on the alert, watching Congress, the State legislature,
the courts, and the movements in other States, it was always
ready, with remonstrance and advice, pecuniary or moral aid,
to help forward the cause for which it was organized.   And it
was doubtless due to that zeal, watchfulness, and wide-spread
influence, that the representatives of Pennsylvania occupied a
position so honorable in their devotion to freedom and the
claims of humanity during the first twenty years under the
Constitution.   But in the American Convention of Abolition
Societies, in 1804, a decline of interest in the cause of emancipation was admitted and deplored, and the absence of delegates and communications from Southern societies was made
the subject of regretful allusion.   In 1809, after an active service of twenty-five years, it declared that "hitherto the ap-
proving voice of the community and the liberal interpretation
of the laws have smoothed the path of duty and promoted a
satisfactory issue to our humane exertions.   At present, however, the sentiments of our fellow-citizens and the decisions of
our courts are less auspicious."

But, in spite of these inauspicious indications, the Pennsylvania Abolition Society toiled bravely on. It made special efforts against kidnapping; educated and secured homes for colored children. It examined laws respecting colored people, noted their defects, and prepared bills for the legislature. It memorialized Congress on the fugitive-slave law and the slave-trade. In 1818 it examined and condemned the colonization scheme, then just inaugurated. In 1819 it appointed a committee to watch the struggle for the admission of Missouri; and in 1820 it obtained from the government a portion of the school fund for colored children. In the same year it memorialized the legislature for the total abolition of slavery in that commonwealth. Three years afterward it sent to Congress an elaborate memorial against Southern laws imprisoning colored seamen; and in 1827 it " succeeded in procuring the erasure of the most obnoxious features " of a fugitive-slave bill introduced into the State legislature. In 1830 it procured a " supplementary law " to the act against kidnapping. Under its lead the American Convention met in Baltimore in 1828, and in Washington in 1829.

In the year 1833 it received a letter from the New Haven Antislavery Society, one of the first of the modern societies on the basis of immediate and unconditional emancipation. This veteran abolition society, which had been the leader in antislavery movements for half a century, cordially welcomed its new coadjutor. It took occasion, however, to refer to " the apathy which has so generally pervaded the United States upon this subject," — " a state of torpor and insensibility." Referring to the year 1794, when a convention of abolition societies was held in Philadelphia, it said, " Since that time we have seen one after another discontinue its labors, until we were left almost alone." From that time the society has continued steadfast in its support of the objects for which it was organized before the formation of the general government. Caring for the lowly ones by such methods as an earnest purpose and the wisdom of experience suggested, it has ever been mindful of the general interests of emancipation. Though long the acknowledged head of movements for the freedom and elevation of the African race, and long among the faith-

4

less found faithful only itself, yet, when the antislavery cause came up under other auspices, and on a basis more clearly defined, and better adapted to meet the exigencies of the country and the race, it gracefully relinquished the lead to those who, with fresher impulses, were but carrying out the aims it had so long and so faithfully pursued.

The New York Abolition Society was formed in January, 1785. Its officers were taken from the most illustrious men of that day in that Commonwealth. John Jay, who had characterized slavery as a crime of "crimson dye," was chosen president, and Alexander Hamilton secretary. Among its earlier acts was the printing, for gratuitous circulation, of the masterly argument of Dr. Hopkins, contained in his dialogue. The legislature of New York had refused, in 1785, to adopt a system of gradual emancipation. This society petitioned that body year after year, until, in 1799, such an act was passed, declaring all children born thereafter to be free, — males on becoming twenty-eight, and females on becoming twenty-five years of age.

The Rhode Island Society was organized in February, 1789. The first meeting for its formation was held at the house of Dr. Hopkins, at Newport, though the organization was completed at Providence. Several gentlemen of Massachusetts, eminent for philanthropy and piety, were members, and a few from other States, among whom was Jonathan Edwards, of Connecticut. Although Rhode Island had provided that all of African descent born after March, 1784, should be free, this society found sufficient scope for its labors in carrying out the objects of its formation, — " the abolition of slavery, the relief of persons unlawfully held in bondage, and for improving the condition of the African race."

In 1790 the Connecticut Abolition Society was formed. Dr. Ezra Stiles, president of Yale College, and Judge Baldwin, were its president and secretary. Though Connecticut, like Rhode Island, had passed an act in 1784 providing for the gradual abolition of slavery, and though there were less than three thousand slaves in the State, yet the strong proslavery feeling and conservative interest which obtained there opened

a wide and important field for its service.   Numbering among
its members some of the best and ablest men of a State which
could then boast of many distinguished for their piety, learning, and political eminence, it labored with zeal and fidelity.

It was before this society that Jonathan Edwards the
younger, in 1791, proclaimed that " every man who cannot
show that his negro hath by his voluntary conduct forfeited
his liberty, is obligated immediately to manumit him."   Here
was clearly promulgated the duty of immediate emancipation,
as distinctly as it has ever been enunciated by any antislavery
writer, orator, or society before or since.   And this is a fact
of some significance, as well as of justice, to some of those
early pioneers in the cause of emancipation, because of the
impression sometimes conveyed that this is a doctrine of more
modern origin.   Nor were the reasons assigned for this pronounced and unequivocal opinion less radical and uncompro-
mising.   " To hold a man," he solemnly avowed, " in a state
of slavery who has a right to his liberty is to be every day
guilty of robbing him of his liberty, or of man-stealing, and is
a greater sin in the sight of God than concubinage or forni-
cation."

Language more expressive of the essential wickedness of
slavery could hardly be employed.   And it is to be remembered that this was the opinion, not only of one of the leading
minds of New England, but of a class of men which held with
him the duty of immediate repentance for sin, and of another
smaller but highly cultivated class which had accepted the new
philosophy of the French school.

An Abolition Society was formed in New Jersey in 1792,
which largely contributed to the extirpation of slavery in that
State.   Such societies were formed in the more Southern and
more proslavery States of Delaware, Maryland, and Virginia.
Belonging to them and their auxiliaries were some of their
most eminent jurists and statesmen.   They labored earnestly,
and looked forward hopefully to the day, then generally anticipated, when slavery would yield to the benign influences of
the Christian religion and of republican institutions, and pass
away.

The Baltimore Abolition Society declared the objects of its association to be founded in "reason and humanity," and on "an avowed enmity to slavery in every form." The Virginia Abolition Society was equally clear and explicit in its avowal that righteousness exalteth a nation; and that slavery is not only an odious degradation, but an outrageous violation of one of the most essential rights of human nature, and utterly "repugnant to the precepts of the Gospel."

These early abolition societies embraced in their membership some of the purest philanthropists, the ripest scholars, most eminent jurists and the honored statesmen of that age. They were deeply imbued with the spirit of liberty, and were loyal to the precepts of Christianity. Ever zealous, earnest, and devoted, they labored effectively in the cause of emancipation and of the general elevation of the African race. For several years national conventions, in which these societies were represented, were annually held. Earnest arguments and appeals were made by these conventions to Congress, to the State legislatures, to the free people of color, and to the country, to aid in the suppression of the slave-trade, the repeal of inhuman statutes, the protection of free persons of color, and the promotion of the general interests of freedom.

The antislavery National Convention of 1795 addressed South Carolina, Georgia, and the people of the United States. The address to South Carolina was written by Jonathan Edwards the younger, a delegate from Connecticut. In that address he made an earnest appeal in favor of "a numerous class of men existing among them deprived of their natural rights and forcibly held in bondage." He called upon them to ameliorate their condition, and to diffuse knowledge among them. He declared, as a necessary consequence of the traffic in man, that "the minds of our citizens are debased and their hearts hardened by contemplating these people only through the medium of avarice or prejudice."

In the address to the people of the United States the Convention distinctly avowed its design to be "the universal emancipation of the wretched Africans who were yet in bondage." It thus appealed to the people of all the States:

" We cannot forbear expressing to you our earnest desire that you will continue without ceasing to endeavor, by every method in your power which can promise any success, to procure either an absolute repeal of all the laws in your State which countenance slavery, or such an amelioration of them as will gradually produce an entire abolition. Yet, even should that great end be happily attained, it cannot put a period to the necessity of further labor. The education of the emancipated — the noblest and most arduous task which we have to perform — will require all our wisdom and virtue, and the constant exercise of the greatest skill and discretion. When we have broken his chains, and restored the African to the enjoyment of his rights, the great work of justice and benevolence is not accomplished. The new-born citizen must receive that instruction, and those powerful impressions of moral and religious truth, which will render him capable and desirous of fulfilling the various duties he owes to himself and to his country. By educating some in the higher branches of science, and all in the useful parts of learning, and in the precepts of religion and morality, we shall not only do away the reproach and calumny so unjustly lavished upon us, but confound the enemies of truth by evincing that the unhappy sons of Africa, in spite of the degrading influence of slavery, are in no wise inferior to the more fortunate inhabitants of Europe and America."

The Convention, in these thorough and radical sentiments, unquestionably represented the views, principles, and purposes of the abolition societies of those days. As a mode of action, they recommended periodical discourses " on the subject of slavery and the means of its abolition "; and they supported their recommendation by considerations' not often exceeded in thoroughness, cogency, and forcible expression. " If to many persons," they say, " who continue the hateful practice of enslaving their fellow-men, were often applied the force of reason and the persuasion of eloquence, they might be awakened to a sense of their injustice and startled with horror at the enormity of their conduct."

While enlightened, liberal, and Christian statesmen and philanthropists believed with Franklin that slavery was " an atrocious debasement of human nature," and desired with Washington to see some plan adopted by which it "could be abolished by law," there was a powerful class, especially in the Carolinas and Georgia, that actively and persistently resisted everything that tended to the destruction of a system which secured to them wealth, social distinction, and political power. It is indeed true, that the best portion of the cultivated and Christian mind of that day saw the essential injustice and enormity of slavery, and the duty of its discontinuance, as clearly as they have ever been seen since. But the uneducated and unreflecting masses, taking counsel of their feelings of indolence and avarice, and of those induced, in the language of Jefferson, by their "quiet and monotonous course of colonial life," largely influenced and led, too, by the dominant class, had little sympathy with these abstract ideas of right, justice, and humanity, and little disposition to legislate in harmony with them. Mr. Jefferson wrote, near the close of life, that he "soon saw that nothing was to be hoped from such"; and he added that, at the first or second session of the Virginia legislature, of which he himself was a member, Colonel Bland, "one of the oldest, ablest, and most respectable members, was denounced as an enemy to his country, and was treated with the greatest indecorum," for moving "a moderate protection of the laws to these people."

Although the leading men of Virginia — Washington, Jefferson, Henry, and Mason — were hostile to slavery, and were pronounced emancipationists, yet so powerful and despotic was the slaveholding class, and so indifferent were the masses of the people, that Washington, writing to Lafayette in 1785, only two years after the close of the war fought in the name of human equality, confessed that "petitions for the abolition of slavery presented to the Virginia legislature could scarcely obtain a hearing." Thus it happened that the same people, speaking in the language of their most humane and cultivated men, — divines, philanthropists, statesmen, and illustrious Revolutionary leaders, — uttered the clear, ringing words of liberty; while by their legislation, under the malign influence of slavery, they gave the lie to these utterances and framed iniquity into law.

CHAPTER III.

SLAVERY IN THE TERRITORIES. — ORDINANCE OF 1787.

Public Domain. — Cessions of Territory by the States. — Mr. Jefferson's proposed Inhibition of Slavery in the Territories. — Ordinance of 1787, reported by Nathan Dane. — Adopted by Congress. — Sanctioned by First Congress under the Constitution. — Efforts to suspend it in Indiana. — Blessings of the Ordinance of 1787. — Cessions of North Carolina and Georgia, with Limitations concerning Slavery. — The Mississippi Territory. — Debate on Mr. Thatcher's Antislavery Amendment.

THE Treaty of Peace, by which the independence of the thirteen British Colonies was acknowledged, was signed at Paris on the 30th of November, 1782. Beyond the western boundaries of the States, and between the 31st and 47th parallels of latitude, lay a vast and fertile territory, conceded to be embraced within the limits of the new Republic. Not only were these rich lands looked to as a source of revenue for the payment of the debt incurred in the War of Independence, but the far-seeing statesmen of that day saw that States carved from this territory would exert a powerful, if not controlling influence in shaping the destinies of the country. To the future of the United States it was then a question of transcendent importance whether it should be organized into free or slave States. Hence, among the first measures of the Continental Congress, after the British forces had left the country, was an effort to fix the condition of this immense public domain.

The States of Massachusetts, Connecticut, New York, Virginia, North Carolina, and Georgia each claimed severally, under their respective charters, a portion of this territory. These claims were warmly opposed by the landless States, which justly held that this territory had been conjointly won, and should therefore inure to the common benefit.

On the first day of March, 1784, Mr. Jefferson presented to the Continental Congress, then assembled in Annapolis, a deed of cession of all the lands claimed by Virginia northwest of the Ohio River. A select committee was appointed, consisting of himself, Mr. Chase of Maryland, and Mr. Howell of Rhode Island; and this committee reported a plan for the government of the territory ceded, or to be ceded. This plan contemplated its ultimate division into seventeen States. It was therein provided that, "after the year of the Christian era 1800, there shall be neither slavery nor involuntary servitude in any of these States, otherwise than in the punishment of crime, whereof the party shall have been duly convicted."

This provision was stricken out on motion of Mr. Spaight of North Carolina, seconded by Mr. Read of South Carolina. It required the votes of nine States to retain it as a part of the ordinance. Only six voted for it, — New Hampshire, Massachusetts, Rhode Island, Connecticut, New York, and Pennsylvania. Maryland, Virginia, and South Carolina voted against it. North Carolina was divided. Delaware and Georgia were not present. Mr. Dick of New Jersey voted to retain it; but as two members were required to give the vote of a State, that State was not represented in the vote. Though sixteen members voted for the prohibition of slavery, and only seven voted against it, yet then, as so often since, slavery, though in a lean minority, gained a victory that should have fallen to the other side. This important measure would have saved to freedom not only the territory of the Northwest, but also Kentucky, Tennessee, Alabama, and Mississippi.

In March, 1785, Rufus King, a delegate from Massachusetts, moved to modify the report made at the previous session, by inserting therein a total and immediate prohibition of slavery; but his motion failed. In July, 1787, a committee, of which Nathan Dane of Massachusetts was chairman, reported an ordinance for the territory northwest of the Ohio, in which there should be neither slavery nor involuntary servitude. With it there was, however, a stipulation for the rendition of fugitive slaves. This ordinance — which consecrated to freedom the fertile territory covered now by the great States of

Ohio, Indiana, Illinois, Michigan, and Wisconsin — was passed on the 13th of July, 1787 ; every State voting for it, Mr. Yates of New York alone voting against it.

In July, 1789, Mr. Fitzsimmons of Pennsylvania reported in the House of Representatives a bill for the government of the territory northwest of the Ohio River, which passed both houses without opposition. This act gave the emphatic sanction of the first Congress under the Constitution to the ordinance of 1787, prohibiting forever slavery in the territory northwest of the Ohio.

But, notwithstanding this prohibition was so solemnly and with such unanimity adopted, the most persistent efforts were subsequently made to give slavery a foothold in that region. After the admission of Ohio as a free State, the remainder of that territory was organized under the name of the Territory of Indiana. Most of its settlers, coming from the slaveholding States, — with their former tastes, habits, and prejudices, — soon memorialized Congress for a temporary suspension of the ordinance. The convention which sent this memorial was held in 1802. Its presiding officer was Governor William Henry Harrison, afterward President of the United States. The memorial was referred by the House to a select committee, of which John Randolph, the brilliant but erratic Virginian, was chairman. This committee reported that it was " highly dangerous and inexpedient to impair a provision wisely calculated to promote the happiness and prosperity of the Northern country." No action was taken, as the session terminated the following day.

In the next Congress the subject was referred to a committee of which Cæsar Rodney of Delaware — afterward Attorney-General of the United States — was made chairman, and it reported in favor of a suspension of the antislavery restriction for a limited time. Early in February, 1806, James M. Garnett of Virginia, from a select committee, made a like report, though, as in the previous case, no action was taken. Another committee was appointed during the next year, of which Mr. Parke, a delegate from the Territory, was chairman, to which was referred a letter from Governor Harrison, with

5

resolves from the Territorial legislature, favoring a temporary suspension of the inhibition. On the 12th of February this committee reported that the ordinance be suspended for ten years from the 1st of January, 1808. Though this was the third report proposing a temporary suspension of the ordinance of 1787, Congress took no action upon either.

Governor Harrison and the legislature again united in a like request, though at this time a portion of the inhabitants remonstrated against granting it. The subject in the Senate was referred to a select committee, consisting of Franklin of North Carolina, Kitchell of New Jersey, and Tiffin of Ohio. On the 13th of November, 1807, this committee reported a resolve, declaring it not expedient to suspend the sixth article of the compact for the government of the territory northwest of the Ohio. This report closed the efforts made by an undoubted majority of the people of the Territory to be at least temporarily relieved from the operation of this ordinance. In this struggle it is to be noted that they had the effective support and hearty co-operation of General Harrison, their governor, whom the nation with so much enthusiasm bore into the Presidential chair in 1840. Had their wishes prevailed, however, and those imperial States been lost to freedom, who can estimate the increased dangers that would have imperilled the nation and darkened its pathway? Who can comprehend the aggravated difficulties which would have attended the then future, but now accomplished, work of emancipation? There is little danger of overestimating the benefits which the ordinance of 1787 has conferred on the Northwest, or the measureless perils from which it saved the land. Its enactment must ever stand as one of the great events of American history, one of the most important achievements in behalf of freedom.

Virginia having retained her claim to the Territory of Kentucky, into which many of her citizens had taken their slaves, a new slave State was early carved out of it and added to the Union. North Carolina, too, laid claim to Western territory, but ceded Tennessee, in 1789, upon the condition that " no regulation made or to be made by Congress should tend to the emancipation of slaves." This deed of cession was laid before the Senate in the winter of 1790, and referred to a committee, of which Oliver Ellsworth, afterward Chief Justice of the Supreme Court, was chairman. He reported a bill accepting the cession, and providing that the ordinance for the government of the Northwest Territory should be applied to this cession, excepting, however, the clause prohibiting slavery. The bill passed the Senate without division ; was briefly debated in the House, and concurred in with little opposition. Slavery had already entered the Territory ; and Congress, consenting with more or less reluctance to the hard conditions imposed, gave assent to its continuance.

Georgia claimed the territory forming subsequently the States of Alabama and Mississippi. She did not promptly follow the example of her sister States in ceding her territorial claims to the general government ; as her cession was not made until the 2d of April, 1802, and then upon the peremptory condition that the ordinance of 1787 " shall, in all its parts, extend to the territory contained in the present cession, the article only excepted which forbids slavery."

Although Georgia had not previously relinquished her claim to the Mississippi territory, still settlements had been made there, and the duty was imposed upon Congress of legislating for the government of the people of that region. In March, 1798, the House of Representatives proceeded to the consideration of the bill for the government of that Territory. It expressly provided that a government similar in all respects to that of the Northwestern Territory should be established, the inhibition of slavery only excepted. Mr. Thatcher of Massachusetts remarking that he intended to make a motion touching the rights of man, moved to strike out the excepting clause. Mr. Harper of South Carolina said that this was not a legitimate mode of supporting the rights of man. The regulation prohibiting slavery in the Northwest was proper ; but it would not be so in Mississippi. It would be a decree of the banishment of all persons settled there, and a decree of the exclusion of all persons intending to go there. Mr. Varnum, of Massachusetts, afterward Speaker of the House, declared that Mr. Harper's remarks showed that he did not wish to support the rights of all men ; for " where there was a disposition to retain a part of our species in slavery there could not be proper respect for the rights of mankind." He looked upon the practice of holding blacks in slavery in this country to be equally criminal with the practice of the Algerines in carrying American citizens into slavery. Mr. Rutledge wished Mr. Thatcher to withdraw his motion. He remarked that one gentleman called these men " property " ; another said, " you hold these men in chains " ; and another declared, " you violate the rights of man," and wished to know if these men were not property, and held as such by the Spanish government.

Mr. Otis of Massachusetts — an early representative of that class of Northern politicians who have always existed in sufficient numbers to betray their section in an emergency, and give to slavery the victory — expressed the hope that Mr. Thatcher would not withdraw his amendment. He desired, he said, that " an opportunity might be given to gentlemen who came from the North to manifest that it was not their disposition to interfere with the South in regard to that species of property." He thought, he said, — and thus invited the very violence he seemed to deprecate, — that if the amendment was adopted that no slavery should exist in the territory it would be not only a sentence of banishment, but of war ; that an immediate insurrection would take place, and that the inhabitants would not be suffered to retire, but would be massacred on the spot.

Mr. Foster, of the same State, thought that if the amendment was not withdrawn, a long debate might be had upon it. To these remarks of his colleagues Mr. Thatcher replied that he should not withdraw his motion. Believing his course to be just, the more it was opposed the more obstinate he should be in its support. Mr. Giles of Virginia then made the suggestion, often repeated since, that if the slaves of other States were permitted to go to the Western States, and thus spread themselves over a larger territory, there would be a greater prospect of ameliorating their condition. Mr. Hartley of

Pennsylvania felt compelled to vote against the amendment, although he desired to gratify the wishes of philanthropists by doing away with the system of slavery altogether.

Mr. Gallatin of Pennsylvania a gentleman of great learning and capacity, who afterward rendered signal service to his country as a financier and diplomatist, maintained that the amendment striking out the provision of the bill which allowed slavery in the Territory, could not be rejected for want of jurisdiction. He confessed he could not see how forbidding slavery in Mississippi could affect it in South Carolina, any more than forbidding it in the Northwest Territory. If the amendment was rejected, slavery was established for that country, not only during its temporary government, but during all the time it should be a State. The number of slaves would become so large, by constant increase, that when the Territory became a State the slaveholders would be able to secure a constitution recognizing and protecting slavery, and thereby making it permanent. Having determined that slavery would be bad policy for the Northwest Territory, he saw no reason for a contrary determination in respect to the Mississippi Territory.

Mr. Nicholas of Virginia thought that the rejection of the amendment would be not only for the interest of the Territory, but of the United States. But Mr. Thatcher firmly declared that he could never be brought to believe that an individual could have a right in anything that tended to the destruction of the government; that he could have a right in any wrong, as " property in slaves was founded in wrong, and never could be right." Slavery " must be put a stop to ; and the sooner it was begun the better." The amendment was lost, only twelve members voting for it. The bill, however, was amended, on motion of Mr. Harper, so as to prohibit the introduction of slavery into the Territory from beyond the limits of the United States.

In this, the first debate in Congress on the question of permitting or excluding slavery in the Territories, members eminent as jurists and statesmen participated. Although they entertained different views of its expediency, none of them questioned or doubted its constitutionality. The power of Congress to prohibit slavery in the Territories was then conceded by the statesmen of the South as well as by the statesmen of the North. The dogma of " no power in Congress to prohibit slavery in the Territories" had not then been invented.

By this legislation the character of all the territory of the United States was then fixed. Mr. Jefferson's proposition, made in 1784, would have prohibited slavery after 1800 in all that territory. It has ever been a source of profound regret to the friends of freedom that his proposition failed. In the light of subsequent events, however, it is not at all clear that more would have been gained to freedom by its adoption than was secured by Mr. Dane's ordinance, which only applied to the Territory northwest of the Ohio River. Had slavery been allowed in the Northwest Territory till the year 1800, a more powerful and persistent effort — and perhaps one more successful — would have been made for its retention than was actually made by the emigrants from the South and the few old French settlers, who, in spite of the ordinance, retained some in servitude, and strove to legalize the system temporarily, and make, if possible, Indiana and Illinois slave States.

After the adoption of the Constitution the slaveholding class, from the Potomac to the Gulf, rapidly increased in wealth, social influence, and political power. Emigrants from those States settled the Territory south of the Ohio, and carried to that region the habits, prejudices, and interests of their section. They might have taken their slaves with them, made slave laws and constitutions, and sought admission into the Union. Perhaps the ordinance itself might have been temporarily, partially, or wholly set aside by the slaveholding class, which obtained control of the Federal government at the beginning of the century, and held it for two generations. While Mr. Jefferson's proviso might and probably would have failed to secure to freedom the territory south of the Ohio, it might have imperilled it in the territory northwest of that river. Mr. Dane's ordinance of 1787 probably won for freedom all that could have been securely held, and will ever stand as one of the grandest achievements in American history.

CHAPTER IV.

COMPROMISES OF THE CONSTITUTION. — SLAVE REPRESENTATION.
— SLAVE-TRADE. — RENDITION OF FUGITIVE SLAVES.

The Failure of the Confederation. — Distress and Discontent of the People. —
Assembling of the Convention to frame a Constitution. — Difficulties and Dangers. — Antagonism between Freedom and Slavery. — Basis of Representation.
— Debates thereon. — Northern and Southern Parties developed. — Slaveholding Interest successful. — Committee of Detail. — Duties on Exports. —
Regulation of Commerce. — Slave-trade. — South Carolina and Georgia demand
its Continuance. — The Bargain. — Slave Representation. — Slave-trade to be
continued Twenty Years. — Rendition of Fugitive Slaves. — The Compromise.
— The Slave Power developed.

WHEN the British forces had been withdrawn from the
country, the American army disbanded, and then, the common
danger removed, other evils revealed themselves and other
dangers menaced. The people were deeply embarrassed by
public and private indebtedness, by a depreciated currency,
and by the general derangement of business, resulting from
an exhausting warfare with the first power of the globe. It
became almost impossible to enforce the collection of debts or
to maintain public order. The distress and discontent of the
people revealed themselves in forcible attempts to obstruct the
action of the judicial tribunals, while the public disorders
threatened anarchy and civil war. Then, too, the Confederation, which had so signally failed to command fully the resour-
ces of the country during the war, more clearly manifested its
weakness. Then the statesmen and soldiers, whose wisdom
and valor had carried the country through the Revolution,
were profoundly concerned at the grave and ominous aspect of
national affairs. Under this pressure of difficulties and dangers, which threatened to defeat and destroy much of what
had been gained and won by the blood and treasure, the hard-

ships and hazards of the contest, a convention was called to revise the Articles of Confederation ; and it gave the country the Constitution of the United States.

The convention assembled at Philadelphia in May, 1787. It was a body of men of marked ability and large experience in public affairs. It embraced many of the Revolutionary leaders, from both council-chamber and field, while among its younger members were several who at once took rank among the foremost public men of the new Republic. Nor did their abilities exceed their necessities, or transcend the greatness of the occasion. To make " a more perfect union " of States so widely scattered on a narrow strip of the Atlantic coast, so diverse in origin and history, so alien in spirit and purpose, so jealous of their own interests and fearful of the encroachments of others, impoverished and distressed by war, might reasonably be expected to disclose difficulties of the gravest import. In forming such a general government, of States so unequal in territory, population, and wealth, there would naturally exist not merely the general reluctance to relinquish their individual prerogatives as independent States, but also the fear of the larger States, that in the government their influence would not be commensurate with their relative size, while the smaller States would hardly be satisfied with a share graduated by any such standard. Their history immediately preceding the assembling of the convention had but aggravated this natural tendency. State rights had been vigilantly guarded, and State power reluctantly relinquished to the Continental Congress, even under the pressing exigencies of war. State pride, too, was intense ; State rivalries and jealousies were active. Consequently, the more thoughtful members of the convention apprehended that the main hindrances in the way of success would spring from such sources, — indeed, that the great difficulty would be to reconcile the differences between the larger and smaller States. The result, however, revealed the fact that all these difficulties were, if not lost, overshadowed by another issue far more serious and threatening. The real obstacle was found in the antagonism between freedom and slavery, between the States which had accepted and were accepting the former and the States which clung with such persistent determination to the latter. Indeed, we have the statement of Mr. Madison himself that " the institution of slavery and its consequences furnished the line of discrimination." Nor, in the lights of the present day and the revelations of the nation's subsequent history, is this at all surprising.

The theory of human equality had been enunciated by the first Continental Congress, and proclaimed in the deathless words of the Declaration of Independence. It had been incorporated into the Bills of Rights of several of the States, and had been illustrated by the judicial proceedings of several of their courts. It was held by some of the most eminent members of the convention, and also by other leading statesmen of that era. But there came into this convention of illustrious men, assembled to frame a constitution for a Christian nation, a powerful minority believing in and representing chattel slavery. In that crisis of the country, — when its very existence was in peril, and the only alternative seemed to be a constitution or anarchy, — that minority made it a condition precedent to their assent that the convention should comply with the exactions of the slaveholding interest. The representatives of that interest, — able, arbitrary, and adroit, — taking advantage of the necessities of the country, wrung from the convention fatal concessions, which then and thereafter trammelled the hand of Liberty and armed the hand of Slavery.

The framers of the Constitution have been sharply criticised for their concessions to the slaveholding interest. These concessions, in direct antagonism with the doctrines of human rights so grandly proclaimed in the Declaration of Independence, greatly embarrassed them then, and have been used with fatal force by the Slave Power in its dominating and aggressive career since. But posterity, remembering the fearful stress of circumstances under which those concessions were made, and recalling the significant question of Alexander Hamilton, " Is it possible to deliberate between anarchy and confusion on one side, and the chance of good on the other ? " will min-

gle large charity with its censure. Whatever may be the
judgments of coming generations, removed from the disturb-
ing and distorting influences of the past and present hour, and
occupying a higher plane of thought and feeling, concerning
the framers of the Constitution and their concessions to the
Slave Power under the terrible pressure to which they were
subjected, it does not become the men of later times, who have
made compromise after compromise, far greater sacrifices of
principle, and far more guilty concessions, with but a tithe of
that pressure resting upon them, to reproach them. Whoever
else may be, they are not the men to cast stones.

There was a great struggle in the convention touching the
basis of representation in Congress, in which the question
of slavery largely mingled. It originated in the strife between the larger and smaller States, the latter contending for
an equal and the former for a proportional representation. The
Virginia plan proposed to base the representation on free inhabitants and three fifths of all other persons. Twice the convention voted in favor of a proportional representation. Having
failed to secure an equal representation in the House, the party
representing the smaller States made a strenuous effort to
secure an equality of representation in the Senate; but the
proposition was defeated by a tie vote. The State-rights members, being defeated, manifested much dissatisfaction.

On motion of Mr. Sherman of Connecticut, a committee of
conference of one from each State was appointed. In this
committee Franklin proposed that the States should be equally
represented in the Senate; while for the House the Virginia
proposition should be adopted, allowing one representative for
forty thousand inhabitants, slaves being counted in the ratio
of three fifths.

It having been determined that the States should not be
equally represented in the House, new questions arose, and
new divisions and parties were developed. A committee, consisting of Morris, Gorham, King, Randolph, and Rutledge, reported a proposition that future representation should be dis-
tributed among the States in a compound proportion of wealth
and numbers. This report was referred to a committee of one

from each State; and this committee reported the temporary apportionment finally introduced into the Constitution, with a House of sixty-five members. Future apportionments, however, could not be easily determined.

Mr. Patterson of New Jersey, one of the leaders of the party of State Rights, opposed the representation of slaves, because it afforded an " indirect encouragement of the slave-trade." He said that Congress, in its acts concerning the quota of troops, was ashamed to use the word " slave," and substituted a description. He could look upon slaves in no other light than as property, and strenuously opposed their representation. In reply, Mr. Madison admitted the soundness of the general principle, but thought it should forever silence the claims of the small States; and he suggested that the House should be based on the whole number of free inhabitants, and the Senate, which represented property, on the whole number, including slaves.

Mr. King expressed the opinion that the Southern States, being the richest, would not league themselves with the Northern unless some attention was paid to their wealth. It was proposed by Mr. Randolph that the future apportionments should be regulated by a periodical census. It was then moved, as a substitute, by Mr. Williamson of North Carolina, to reckon in the census the freemen, and three fifths of all other persons. It was strenuously insisted by Pierce Butler and Charles C. Pinckney, of South Carolina, that slaves should be counted like all other persons. Mr. Williamson's proposition was supported by Mr. Gorham and Mr. Gerry, of Massachusetts. It was insisted by Mr. Butler that the labor of a slave in South Carolina is as productive as that of a freeman in Massachusetts; that slaves are as valuable to the nation as freemen, and that an equal representation ought to be allowed.

Mr. Mason of Virginia thought slaves ought not to be excluded in the basis of representation; but that they were not equal to freemen. The three-fifths clause was stoutly opposed by Mr. Morris, as " an encouragement to the slave-trade, an injustice to human nature." Mr. Wilson of Pennsylvania was apprehensive that the people of his State would be disgusted

by this " blending of blacks and whites." He thought, if slaves
were admitted as citizens, they should be admitted on an equality with other citizens ; but if as property, then, he asked, why
not admit them as other property ? Mr. Butler's amendment
to count slaves equally with free persons was lost, — Delaware,
South Carolina, and Georgia only voting for it. Mr. Williamson's substitute, basing the House on a periodical census of the
inhabitants, slaves being counted in the ratio of three fifths,
was defeated, — Massachusetts, New Jersey, Delaware, Maryland, and South Carolina voting against it. South Carolina
voted against it because she demanded an equal representation
for slaves. The proposition of Mr. Randolph for a periodical
census was also defeated. It was then unanimously agreed,
on motion of Mr. Morris, that taxation should be in proportion
to representation.

Up to this point, though the struggle had been sharp, slavery
had rather lost than gained. The three propositions — to count
the slaves according to their numbers, to count them in the ratio
of three fifths, and to have a periodical census taken — had
been lost. The proposition now before the convention was to
base all future apportionments upon the compound ratio of
wealth and numbers. As parliamentary eloquence and tactics
had not succeeded, something more stringent was demanded.
The soft words of persuasion had failed ; the virtue of stones
must be tried. The ever-present and ever-potent argument of
the plantation — the whip — must be put in requisition. Nor
did it fail. The recusant members were at once brought to
terms, and the fatal lesson was taught and learned which was
not forgotten for nearly three quarters of a century.

General Davie of North Carolina, who had been a silent
member to that time, arose and emphatically declared, " It is
time to speak out. I see," he said, " that it is meant by
some gentlemen to deprive the Southern States of any representation of their blacks. I am sure that North Carolina will
never confederate on any terms that do not rate them at least as
three fifths. If the Eastern States mean to exclude them altogether, then the business is at an end." The menace was
effective, and secured at once what no amount of debate had

accomplished. Mr. Johnson of Connecticut at once arose and hastened to declare that the whole population should be counted. Mr. Randolph renewed the proposition to count slaves as three fifths in the basis of representation. The proposition was now carried, — Connecticut, Pennsylvania, Maryland, Virginia, North Carolina, and Georgia voting for it ; New Jersey and Delaware opposing it ; while Massachusetts and South Carolina divided. By this vote it was provided that the half a million slaves in the five Southern States, and their increase in coming years, should be counted in the basis of representation in the House, and in the Electoral College, in the ratio of three fifths.

Thus, by this most illogical measure, by which votes were given, in effect, to a portion of the community from which not only the right of citizenship, but all rights, were studiously withheld, — and these votes not to be cast by themselves, and for their benefit, but by their masters, for their injury, — large power was placed in the hands of the slaveholding class, which was long used with terrible effect for its aggrandizement and the nation's harm. In many of the sharply contested and evenly balanced struggles between the friends and foes of freedom it gave the latter the needed majority and turned the scale against the cause of justice. In the great struggle of 1820, to make Missouri free, it gave to slavery its victory ; and in that of 1854, to remove the landmarks of freedom, its power for evil was equally decisive. In 1800 it decided the presidential election, and gave it to the slaveholding Democracy, and thus enthroned the Slave Power in the General Government, from which it was never dislodged until the election of Mr. Lincoln.

On the 24th of July a Committee of Detail was appointed, consisting of Rutledge, Randolph, Gorham, Ellsworth, and Wilson. To this committee was referred the work of the convention, embodied in twenty-three resolutions, and the propositions offered by Mr. Charles Pinckney of South Carolina, and also of Mr. Patterson of New Jersey. Mr. Charles C. Pinckney, one of the most eminent men of that age, the very embodiment and exponent of the rising Slave Power, perhaps emboldened by the success of the member from North Carolina, rose and pronounced another ultimatum of Southern demands. He reminded the convention that if it did not provide proper security for Southern interests he should vote against whatever report the committee should bring in. In other words, it was a notice to the convention that the South would demand not only an enumeration of slaves in the basis of representation, but the right to continue their importation without taxation, and such other guaranties as the exigencies of their peculiar institution demanded.

On the 6th of August the Committee of Detail brought in its report. It was in substance a sketch of the Constitution as finally adopted. It provided that no duty should be laid on exports, and that no navigation acts should be passed except by a two-thirds vote. The importation of slaves was not to be prohibited ; neither was any tax to be imposed upon such importation. Those provisions were wholly in the interest of the slaveholders. The exports of rice, tobacco, and indigo — products of slave labor — were not to be taxed. Slaves were to be imported untaxed and without hindrance from the Federal government. Foreign vessels were to enter Southern ports and carry Southern products unembarrassed by any discriminating duties in favor of Northern shipping.

The avarice, the ambition, and the sagacity of the slaveholding interest have never been more clearly revealed than in this report of the Committee of Detail. At its head stood John Rutledge, who completely embodied the pride, arrogance, and dominating characteristics of the extreme South, and who needed no hint from his colleague to watch over and guard its interests. Had the subtle and adroit policy of that report been fully indorsed and adopted by the convention and the people, the ascendency of the slave States, and the consequent humiliation and helplessness of the free States, would have been complete.

The first Continental Congress, in the Articles of Association, had pledged the united colonies against the importation of slaves ; and the Congress of 1776, in releasing the colonies from some of the provisions of the Articles of Association, had resolved that " no slave be imported into any of the United States." Most of the States had united in prohibiting the slave-trade. North Carolina had imposed a duty on importations ; while South Carolina and Georgia were in favor, not only of perpetuating slavery, but also of continuing the slave-traffic. Some Northern merchants, forgetful of the pledges of the government, still employed their ships in the hateful trade. Two years before the assembling of the convention, Dr. Samuel Hopkins had stated that portions of the people were " going into the practice of that sevenfold abomination, the slave-trade." While Maryland and Virginia agreed with the slave-holders of South Carolina and Georgia against taxing exports, the products of slave labor, and were opposed to navigation laws for the encouragement of the shipping interest, they were opposed — it is hardly uncharitable to believe, for the twofold reason that they did not need foreign slaves, and were themselves engaged in the domestic slave-traffic — to the reopening and continuance of the African slave-trade. Consequently the slaveholding class was not a unit in supporting the report of the Committee of Detail.

That report, dictated by the Carolinas and Georgia, deeply aroused the feelings of delegates from the free States. Mr. King of Massachusetts took the earliest opportunity to denounce " the admission of slaves " into the basis of apportionment. He stated that by the report of the committee " the importation of slaves could not be prohibited, and exports could not be taxed " ; that " there was so much inequality and unreasonableness in all this that the people of the North could never be reconciled to it. He never could agree to let slaves be imported without limitation, and then be represented in the national legislature. Either slaves should not be represented, or exports should be taxable."

Gouverneur Morris followed in an eloquent denunciation of slavery, emphatically declaring that " it was a nefarious institution ; it was the curse of Heaven on the States where it prevailed." " Upon what principle is it," he asked, " that the slaves shall be computed in the representation ? Are they

men ? Then make them citizens, and let them vote. Are
they property ? Why, then, is no other property included ?
The houses in this city are worth more than all the wretched
slaves that cover the rice-swamps of South Carolina." He
declared that the inhabitants of the South, who went to the
coast of Africa, and, in defiance of the sacred laws of humanity, tore away their fellow-creatures, and damned them to the
most cruel bondage, had more power than the citizens of the
North, who viewed with horror a practice so nefarious. He
added " that domestic slavery is the most prominent feature
in the aristocratic countenance of the proposed Constitution.
The vassalage of the poor has ever been the favorite offspring
of the aristocracy. And what is the proposed compensation
to the Northern States for a sacrifice of every principle of
right, every impulse of humanity ? They are to bind themselves to march their militia, for the defence of the Southern
States, against those very slaves. The Southern States are
not to be restrained from importing fresh supplies of wretched
Africans at once to increase the danger of attack and the difficulty of defence ; nay, they are to be encouraged to it by
having their votes in the national government increased in
proportion, and at the same time to have their slaves and
exports exempt from all contributions to the public service."
He then emphatically avowed that he would " sooner submit
himself to a tax for paying for all the slaves in the United
States than to saddle posterity with such a constitution." He
closed his speech by moving to confine the basis of representation to free inhabitants.

Roger Sherman opposed the motion ; and, in doing it, made
the very extraordinary declaration, for a New England man,
that he " did not regard the admission of negroes as liable to
such insuperable objections." Charles Pinckney, in reply to
Mr. Morris, asserted that he could demonstrate that the fisher-
ies and the Western frontiers were more burdensome than the
slaves. Mr. Morris's motion was rejected, New Jersey alone
voting for it.

When the clause came up forbidding any restrictions on the
importation of slaves, Luther Martin of Maryland moved an

amendment, allowing such importation to be taxed. He stated that, as five slaves were equal to three freemen, the permission to import them was an encouragement of the slave-trade. " Slaves," he said, " weakened the Union which other parts are bound to protect. The privilege of importing them is, therefore, unreasonable. Such a feature in the Constitution is inconsistent with the principles of the Revolution, and dishonorable to the American character."

Mr. Rutledge, chairman of the committee, declared that he " did not see how this section would encourage the importation of slaves." In reply to the assertion that the Union was to protect the slaves, he said that he would " readily exempt the other States from every obligation to protect the South." He averred that "religion and humanity have nothing to do with this question. Interest alone is the governing principle with nations. The true question is, whether the Southern States shall or shall not be parties to the Union." Thus the issue was distinctly made by the chairman of the Committee of Detail, that the Southern States would enter the Union only on the condition that the African slave-trade should be continued. Appealing to commercial cupidity, he said that, if the Northern States consulted their own interest, they would not oppose the increase of slaves, because it would increase the commodities of which they would become the carriers. Nor was the appeal without effect.

Mr. Ellsworth, a member of the committee, immediately avowed himself in favor of the provision as it stood. " Let every State," he said, " import what it pleases. The morality or wisdom of slavery are considerations belonging to the States. What enriches a part enriches the whole, and the States are the best judges of their particular interests. The old confederation had not meddled with this point; and he did not see any greater necessity for bringing it into the policy of the new one."

Charles Pinckney, speaking for the slaveholding class, emphatically asserted : " South Carolina can never receive the plan, if it prohibits the slave-trade. In every proposed extension of the powers of Congress, that State has expressly and

7

watchfully excepted the power of meddling with the importa-
.tion of negroes."

George Mason of Virginia strongly denounced the slave-
trade, laying the blame of it on the avarice of British merchants, and lamenting that his Eastern brothers had from
the lust of gain embarked in the traffic. " Slavery," he said,
" discourages arts and manufactures. The poor despise labor
when performed by slaves. It prevents the emigration of
whites, who really enrich and strengthen the country. It pro-
.duces the most pernicious effects on manners, — every master
of slaves is born a petty tyrant. It brings the judgment of
Heaven on a country. By an inevitable chain of causes and
effects, Providence punishes national sins by national calami-
ties." He then avowed that he held it essential in every point
of view that the general government should have power to
prevent the increase of slavery.

Mr. Ellsworth thought that, if the question was to be viewed
in a moral light, the convention should go further, and free
those already in the country. In Maryland and Virginia it
was cheaper to raise than to import; but in the sickly rice-
swamps, he coldly said, foreign importation was necessary, and
it would be unjust to South Carolina and Georgia to prohibit
their importation. " Let us not," he said, " intermeddle. As
population increases, poor laborers will be so plenty as to render slaves useless. Slavery in time will not be a speck in our
country."

Mr. Sherman joined Mr. Ellsworth in allowing the clause as
reported by the committee to stand. Charles C. Pinckney
avowed that " South Carolina and Georgia cannot do without
slaves. As to Virginia, she will gain by stopping importation.
Her slaves will rise in value, and she has more than she wants.
It would be unfair to ask South Carolina and Georgia to confederate on such unequal terms." The importation of slaves, he
maintained, would be for the benefit of the whole Union. The
more slaves, the more produce ; the greater carrying trade, the
more consumption, the more revenue. The delegation from
South Carolina united in the emphatic declaration that, if the
slave-trade was prohibited, South Carolina would not come into

the Union. Mr. Baldwin of Georgia, too, avowed that his State would not confederate unless she were allowed to import slaves ; and Mr. Williamson joined in expressing the opinion that, if South Carolina and Georgia were not allowed to import slaves, they would not become members of the Union. Mr. Wilson of Pennsylvania suggested that, "if negroes were the only imports not subject to a duty, such an exception would amount to a bounty." Gerry of Massachusetts and Langdon of New Hampshire would give no sanction whatever to the slave-trade.

Mr. King thought the exemption of slaves from duty, while every other import was subject to it, was an inequality that could not fail to strike the commercial sagacity of the Northern and Middle States. Mr. Charles Pinckney hastened to move a recommitment, with a view to a tax on slaves equal to a tax imposed on other imports. His motion was seconded by Mr. Rutledge, his colleague. It was proposed by Gouverneur Morris that the clauses relating to navigation laws and taxation on exports should be referred, making the significant and pregnant suggestion that "these things may form a *bargain* between the Northern and Southern States." The commitment was supported by Mr. Randolph, who avowed that he would rather risk the Constitution than support the clause as it stood. Mr. Sherman said that a tax on slaves implied that they were property ; and Mr. Ellsworth continued to support the article as reported by the committee. The motion to commit prevailed, and the matter was referred to a committee of one from each State. This committee made " a bargain," and reported it. The prohibition of export duties was retained, the restriction of the enactment of navigation laws was stricken out, and the slave-trade permitted till 1800, subject to the imposition of such a duty on slaves as Congress might determine.

This report was supported by Mr. Williamson and Mr. Gorham ; but the tax was objected to by Mr. Sherman, because it implied that slaves were property, and because the tax was too small to discourage importation. But Mr. Gorham replied that the tax should be regarded, not as implying that men were property, but as a discouragement to their importation. Mr.

Madison " thought it wrong to admit into the Constitution the idea that there could be property in man," and a change was therefore made in the phraseology to remove that objection.

Mr. Charles C. Pinckney moved to extend the time of the slave-trade from 1800 to 1808. This motion was seconded by Mr. Gorham of Massachusetts, and was carried by the votes of New Hampshire, Massachusetts, Connecticut, Georgia, and South Carolina; against the votes of New Jersey, Pennsylvania, Delaware, and Virginia. The restriction on the enactment of navigation laws was then stricken out; and Charles C. Pinckney, Mr. Butler, and Mr. Rutledge gave the vote of South Carolina in favor of striking out the restrictions, because of the liberal conduct of the Eastern States in giving them twenty years of extension to the slave-trade.

Thus New Hampshire, Massachusetts, and Connecticut stand on the record as parties to a dishonorable and humiliating " bargain," by which, for a mere commercial consideration, — the removal of all restriction on Congress to enact navigation laws, — they gave twenty years to the African slave-traffic, unrestrained by national legislation. Opposition to giving Congress power to encourage, develop, and protect the commercial and navigating interest of the nation sprung from the narrowness, jealousy, and all-pervading selfishness of slaveholding society. Statesmanship demanded that such restrictions should be excluded from the organic law of a free and commercial nation. Duty to their own section, to their whole country, required that the delegates from New England should resist the incorporation of that plantation policy into the Constitution they were framing for a continental empire. But it will ever be a matter of regret, as well as of reproach, that those New England States achieved their success by a surrender of principles in accord alike with the dictates of humanity and the divine precepts of the Christian religion. And, as men correctly apprehend the true nature of that " bargain," the real significance and true value of Mr. Pinckney's damaging words of praise will be appreciated, when he declared that " he had had prejudices against the Eastern States before he came here ; but he would acknowledge that he had found them as liberal and candid as any men whatever." Nor will the record seem any more flattering because other extreme Southern men joined in that commendation.

It will be remembered that when the Committee of Detail was appointed, to which were referred the results then reached by the convention, Charles C. Pinckney rose and reminded the body that, if the committee failed to insert some provision against the abolition of slavery, he should be bound by the duty he owed South Carolina to vote against its report. At that time slavery had disappeared, or was disappearing, in the seven Northern States, where it never had to any great extent existed; but there were more than half a million of slaves in Maryland, Virginia, North Carolina, South Carolina, and Georgia. While many of the most eminent men of those States, especially of Virginia, believed slavery to be in every form an evil, and desired the inauguration of a system of emancipation; the body of the people, influenced by pecuniary interests, and the pride, passion, and prejudices of race, were in favor of its continuance. Statesmen, quick to discover the drift of public sentiment, were then beginning to look to the slaveholding interest as an element of political power. In the work of obtaining securities for slavery the able statesmen South Carolina sent to the convention took the lead. She could enter no union, they said, accept no constitution, unless slaves should enter into the basis of representation, the slave-trade be continued, and provision be made for the rendition of slaves escaping from their masters.

But the Committee of Detail reported no provision for the rendition of fugitive slaves. When the article came under consideration providing that the citizens of each State should be entitled to all the privileges and immunities of the citizens of the several States, Mr. Pinckney again demanded a provision "in favor of property in slaves." The article, however, was adopted without any such clause.

When the article respecting fugitives from justice escaping from one State into another came up for consideration, Mr. Butler, on behalf of South Carolina, moved to require "fugitive slaves and servants to be delivered up like criminals."

This amendment was objected to by Mr. Wilson, for the inconsequential reason that it would require the delivery to be made at the public expense; while Mr. Sherman remarked, with little more appreciation of the magnitude of the question involved, that he saw " no more propriety in the public seizing and surrendering a servant than a horse." Mr. Butler then withdrew his amendment, for the purpose of putting it in a new form. But the next day, the 29th of August, he introduced it, and it was agreed to without a division.

This provision was inserted in the Constitution for the express purpose of securing what did not exist under the Articles of Confederation, — the rendition of slaves escaping from one State into another. General Pinckney, the exponent of that class of slaveholders who were in favor of the perpetuity of the slavery of the African race, demanded this provision as a condition precedent to the adoption of the Constitution; and the convention yielded. In the convention of South Carolina for its ratification General Pinckney emphatically declared : " We have a right to recover our slaves in whatever part of America they may take refuge. In short, considering all circumstances, we have made the best terms for the security of this species of property it was in our power to make. We would have made better, if we could ; but, on the whole, I do not think them bad." It was stated by Mr. Madison, in the convention of Virginia, that " this clause was expressly inserted to enable owners of slaves to reclaim them." It was stated, too, in the North Carolina Convention, by Mr. Iredell, afterward judge of the Supreme Court of the United States, that, though the word " slave " was not mentioned, owing to the peculiar scruples of Northern delegates on the subject of slavery, the article was inserted to enable masters to recover their slaves escaping into other States.

Thus was incorporated into the Constitution that fearful and far-reaching provision which actually transformed the whole territory of the Republic into one vast hunting-ground, in which brutal men — such as slavery alone can make — might range at pleasure, and, under cover of the cruel and inhuman statutes it authorized, hunt, seize, and return to bondage men and women whose only crimes were a desire to be free and a heroism to dare the perils of escape for that priceless boon ; while their friends, and the friends of justice and humanity, could only look on, impotent for help, blushing at their country's degradation, and sympathizing, though vainly, with its victims. The only palliation to be urged for thus yielding to the wicked demands and the imperious threats of slave-masters was the weakness of faith and courage naturally arising from the perils menacing the country, and the too confident expectation that slavery was to be but a temporary system, soon to pass away.

From the opening of the War of the Revolution to the meeting of the convention, the supporters of slavery had moved with hesitating step. The clash of arms, and the enunciation of the primal truth of human rights in the Declaration of Independence, in the constitutions of several of the States, and by eminent statesmen and philanthropists, threatened the security and perpetuity of the system. Action against the slave-trade, emancipation in several of the Northern States, the permission of Virginia to humane masters to give freedom to their slaves, the plan devised, but not adopted, for gradual emancipation in Virginia by Thomas Jefferson and George Wythe, the ordinance inhibiting slavery in the vast territory northwest of the Ohio, showed the tendencies of the age, weakened the confidence of slaveholders in the stability of their system, while at the same time they begot a too credulous expectation among the friends of freedom of its speedy downfall.

But the incorporation of the fatal concessions to slavery into the fundamental law of the nation breathed into the system new life, and inspired new hope in those desirous of its indefinite perpetuation. Little did the men of that convention comprehend the full significance of their action in the added vitality which these concessions imparted to the slave system. Little did they anticipate the stimulus which would be given to it by a stable government, the opening of fresh territory, and the large increase of the cotton culture. Little did they foresee the wonderful growth and expansion of a system that was to poison the fountain of national life and diffuse its pestiferous influences throughout the land. Nor did they at all realize that even then they were bowing before a new-born power, which would for more than two generations pervert the government from the very purposes for which they were establishing it, until at last it should perish in the vain attempt to compass its overthrow.

CHAPTER V.

PROPOSED TAX ON SLAVES. — FIRST SLAVERY DEBATES IN CON-
GRESS. — PETITIONS FOR EMANCIPATION. — POWERS OF THE
GOVERNMENT DEFINED.

Meeting of Congress. — Proposition to tax Slaves Imported. — Debate on the
Amendment. — Defeat of the Proposition. — Petitions for Emancipation. —
Franklin's Memorial. — Excited Debate. — Special Committee. — Report of
the Committee. — Southern Members defend Slavery and the Slave-trade. —
Tone of the Debate. — Powers of Congress defined and declared. — Mr. Mif-
flin's Petition. — Right of Petition violated.

THE first Congress under the Constitution met in the city of
New York, in March, 1789; though a quorum did not appear
until the 6th of April. It at once addressed itself to the
pressing duty of organizing the new government, and of providing means for its support. When the bill imposing a duty
on imports was under consideration in the House of Representatives, Mr. Parker of Virginia moved an amendment,
imposing a duty of ten dollars on every slave imported.
This amendment excited much interest, especially among the
members from South Carolina and Georgia. Mr. Smith, of
the former State, hastened to express the hope "that such
an important and serious proposition would not be hastily
adopted"; and he averred that "no one topic had been yet
introduced so important to South Carolina and the welfare of
the Union."

Roger Sherman of Connecticut expressed his approval of
"the object of the motion, but did not think it a fit subject to
be embraced in this bill. He could not reconcile himself to
the insertion of human beings as a subject of import among
goods, wares, and merchandise." He then earnestly urged
the withdrawal of the amendment, and suggested that it might
afterward be introduced as an independent proposition.

8

Mr. Jackson of Georgia declared that he was "not surprised, however others might be, at the quarter whence this motion came. Virginia, an old settled State, has her complement of slaves, and, the natural increase being sufficient for her purpose, she was careless of recruiting her numbers by importation. But gentlemen ought to let their neighbors get supplied before they imposed such a burden." He expressed his confidence that, on account of the unsuitableness of the motion to the business in hand, it would be withdrawn. Alluding petulantly to the "white slaves" "imported from all the jails of Europe," he contended that they should be "equally taxed" with the African, and that such a course would be equally constitutional and proper.

To the suggestion of withdrawing the amendment, Mr. Par-. ker — who had, on moving it, expressed his regret that the Constitution prevented Congress from prohibiting altogether the importation of slaves — declared that, "having introduced the motion on mature reflection, he did not like to withdraw it." He proceeded further, and expressed the hope that "Congress would do all in their power to restore to human nature its inherent privileges; to wipe off, if possible, the stigma under which America labored; to do away the inconsistency in our principles justly charged upon us; and to show by our actions the purer beneficence of the doctrine held out to the world in our Declaration of Independence."

Mr. Sherman again avowed his opposition to the amendment, as it was inconsistent with the principle of the bill, which was to raise revenue, while the principle of the amendment was to correct a moral evil. Fisher Ames of Massachusetts expressed his detestation of "slavery from his soul; but he had some doubts whether imposing a duty on such importation would not have an appearance of countenancing the practice."

Mr. Jackson further opposed the amendment. "It is," he said, "the fashion of the day to favor the liberty. of slaves. I believe that they are better off as they are, and better off than they were in Africa. Experience has shown that liberated slaves will not work for a living." He then asked if Virginia would free her negroes, and declared that "when the practice comes to be tried, then the sound of liberty will lose those charms which make it grateful to the ravished ear."

The amendment was supported by Mr. Bland of Virginia, who expressed the wish that slavery had never been introduced into America, and was willing to join in any measure to prevent its extending further. Mr. Madison said that the clause in the Constitution allowing a tax was inserted, he believed, "for the purpose of enabling Congress to give some testimony of the sense of America with respect to the African trade. By expressing a national disapprobation of that trade, it is to be hoped we may destroy it, and so save ourselves from reproaches and our posterity from the imbecility ever attendant upon a country filled with slaves. This is as much the interest of Carolina and Georgia as of any other State. Every addition they receive to their number of slaves tends to weakness and renders them less capable of self-defence. In case of hostility with other nations, their slave population will be a means, not of repelling invasion, but of inviting attack. It is the duty of the general government to protect every part of the Union against danger, as well internal as external. Everything, therefore, which tends to increase this danger, though it might be a local affair, yet, if it involves national expense or safety, becomes of concern to any part of the Union, and a proper subject for the consideration of those charged with the general administration of the government."

These views of Mr. Madison were humane, just, comprehensive, and statesmanlike. Had they been generally entertained and adhered to by Southern statesmen, and accepted by the Southern people, the amelioration, restriction, and extinction of slavery, rather than its expansion and perpetuation, would have been their chosen policy. But widely differing counsels prevailed. Not only the nation, indeed, but Mr. Madison himself, and the class of Southern men he represented, failed to employ the powers here enunciated in behalf of freedom and humanity, or to maintain the humane sentiments here avowed. They soon yielded to the force of circumstances, for which they had not calculated, and which they seemed powerless to control; and became, if not the advocates, the consenting witnesses to the aggressive encroachments and assaults on human rights. They had not anticipated and were not prepared for the soon disclosed fact, that to the ordinary motives for the continued existence of slavery there were to be added the stimulus of the greatly increased industries developed and fostered by the new government. Nor had they then realized how exacting and tyrannous the slave-masters, flushed with their successes in the convention, would soon become, and with what tenacity and persistency they would press the advantages they then gained. They had faint conceptions of the concessions made in the Constitution to the slave interest. For from the time they were made the demands of consistency and the logic of those concessions were always against them. Consenting to the great wrong, they lost too much of their moral power. Leaving the rock of principle, they found no foothold on the shifting sands of expediency and compromise, on which they could stand against the compact forces of the Slave Power, however vile and desperate its cause might be. Ever after these fatal concessions in the Constitution the nation seemed like a strong man struggling in toils and meshes; or, rather, like the giant shorn of his locks, sleeping in the lap of the wanton who had lured him to dishonor, if not to destruction.

At the suggestion of Mr. Madison Mr. Parker withdrew his amendment, with the understanding that it should be afterward brought up as a distinct measure. The subject was subsequently referred to a committee, of which he was made chairman. He reported a bill which was referred to the next session; but it was never acted upon. The men who extorted from the framers of the Constitution the permission to continue the slave-trade for twenty years were in no mood to allow a tax of ten dollars on every imported African. They were not only jealous of any action on the part of the Federal government, but they determined to secure the full benefits of the traffic in human flesh.

Within one year after the organization of the first Congress, memorials were presented deploring the evils of slavery and praying for immediate action for their abatement. They revealed a deep sense of justice, a high regard for the rights of man, and a profound recognition of the claims of morality and religion. On the 11th of February, 1790, a petition was presented from the Quakers to the House of Representatives. The memorialists alluded to the fact that " the same religious society addressed, in 1783, the then Congress on the same subject; which body, though the Christian rectitude of the concern was by the delegates generally acknowledged, yet, not being vested with the powers of legislation, declined " acting on the subject. They say : " As professors of faith in that ever-blessed, all-perfect Lawgiver, whose injunction remains of undiminished obligation, — ' Whatsoever ye would that men should do unto you, do ye even so unto them ' ; and firmly believing that unfeigned righteousness in public as well as private citizens is the only sure ground of hope of the divine blessing ; . . . . we feel it incumbent on us, as a religious body, to attempt to excite your attention to the affecting subject," and induce you to " exert your upright endeavors to the full extent of your power." They expressed the confident expectation that the exercise of that power " must produce the abolition of the slave-trade."

Mr. Hartley of Pennsylvania moved that a petition coming from " so numerous and respectable a part of the community " should be referred to a committee. To this motion Mr. Smith of South Carolina objected ; saying, however respectable the petitioners were, there were others, equally respectable, opposed to their object. Mr. Parker of Virginia expressed his pleasure that " so many were attending to matters of such momentous concern to the future happiness and prosperity of the people." Mr. Madison thought it proper to receive and consider the petition, " because, if there is anything within the Federal authority to restrain such violation of the rights of nature and of mankind, it should be done." But Mr. Stone of Maryland declared it " unfortunate that religious sects seemed to imagine that they understood the rights of human nature better than all the world besides " ; and Mr. Burke of South Carolina, referring contemptuously to some Quakers present, said, " The men in the galleries were meddling with

what did not belong to them; and, though he had great respect for the Quakers, he did not think they had more virtue
and religion than many others, perhaps not so much as some
others."

Mr. Jackson of Georgia, an Englishman by birth, an officer
in the Revolutionary army, and a delegate to the convention
which framed the Constitution, wanted " to know if the whole
morality of the world is confined to the Quakers ? Do they
understand the rights of mankind and the disposition of mankind better than others ? The Saviour had more benevolence
and commiseration than they pretend to have, and he admitted
slavery." Mr. Gerry maintained the right of petition, and
defended the action of the Society of Friends, who wished to
see measures pursued by every nation to wipe off the indelible
stain brought upon all who were concerned in it. The memorial was finally laid upon the table, and thus ended the first
debate on antislavery petitions in Congress.

On the 12th of February, 1790, a memorial was presented
from the " Pennsylvania Society for Promoting the Abolition
of Slavery " signed and said to have been written by Franklin.
As this illustrious citizen died soon afterward, the American
people are justified in regarding it as the last and wisest of
the many sage counsels bequeathed by him to his countrymen.
After alluding to the origin, objects, and general constituency
of the society, being " of various religious denominations," and
to the gratifying circumstance that similar associations were
forming at home and abroad, the memorial proceeds : " That
mankind are all formed by the same Almighty Being, alike
objects of his care and equally designed for the enjoyment of
happiness, the Christian religion teaches us to believe, and the
political creed of Americans fully coincides with that position."
It quotes, too, from the preamble of the Constitution, as indi-
cating one of the objects of that instrument for promoting " the
welfare and securing the blessings of liberty to the people of
the United States," which " blessings of liberty," it declares,
" ought rightfully to be administered without distinction of
color." " From a persuasion, too," it continues, " that equal
liberty was originally the portion and is still the birthright of all

men, we earnestly entreat your serious attention to the subject of slavery ; that you will be pleased to countenance the restoration to liberty of those unhappy men who, alone in this land of freedom, are degraded to perpetual bondage, and who, amidst the general joy of surrounding freemen, are groaning in servile subjection ; that you will devise means for removing this inconsistency from the character of the American people ; . . . . and that you will step to the very verge of power vested in you for discouraging every species of traffic in the persons of our fellow-men."

The memorial of the preceding day was called up, and both were made the subject of an able and exciting debate. Mr. Tucker of South Carolina was " surprised to see another memorial upon the same subject, and that signed by a man who ought to have known the Constitution better." The argument, so often repeated since, was urged, that the movement would aggravate the very evil it was sought to ameliorate and remove, by buoying up the slave with hopes which must be disappointed, and necessitating a severity which would not otherwise be required. He parried the religious argument of the memorial by urging the indorsement of the Southern clergy, who, he said, did not condemn either slavery or the slave-trade. This damaging reference was only too well deserved, and too significant of their subsequent and disastrous course, even up to and throughout the Rebellion. With few exceptions, they failed as religious teachers of educating the people up to the standard of a scriptural morality, shirked the duties imposed upon them by the claims of patriotism, humanity, and religion, betrayed their sacred trust, and proved recreant alike to the claims of benevolence and the Word of God. The weapons they should have pointed against the cruel and wicked system they turned in its defence. Omniscience alone can estimate how much of the subsequent guilt, suffering, and even the destruction of the South was due to their influence who thus early became the blind leaders of the blind. There were not wanting, likewise, at that early date, those who urged the same arguments on which so many changes have been rung since, — the same deprecatory allusions to the danger of discussion, the same reminders of the compromises on which alone the Union was or could have been based. Mr. Baldwin of Georgia, a native of Connecticut, and one of the framers of the Constitution, reminded members that this was " a subject of a most delicate nature " ; that in the convention " the Southern States were so tender upon this point that they had wellnigh broken up without coming to any determination." It was emphatically declared by Mr. Smith of South Carolina, that the Southern " States would never have entered the Confederation unless their property had been guaranteed to them." " When we entered into this Confederacy," he said, " we did it from political and not from moral motives. And I don't think my constituents want to learn morals from the petitioners. I don't believe they want improvement in their moral systems. If they do, they can learn it at home."

On the other hand, Mr. Scott of Pennsylvania defended the memorialists, and condemned in strong and unequivocal language the slave traffic. " I look upon the slave-trade," he said, " to be one of the most abominable things on earth ; and, if there were neither God nor Devil, I should oppose it on principles of humanity and the law of humanity. I cannot, for my part, conceive how any person can be said to acquire property in another. Perhaps in our legislative capacity we can go no further than impose a duty of ten dollars. I do not know how far I might go if I was one of the judges of the United States, and these people were to come before me and claim their emancipation ; but I am sure I would go as far as I could."

To these humane and noble utterances Mr. Jackson of Georgia replied : " If that gentleman is guided by religion, he will find that it is not against it. He will see, from Genesis to Revelation, the current setting strong the other way." In reply to his declaration, that if he were a judge he would go as far as he could in emancipating the people, he said : " I believe that his judgment would be of short duration in Georgia ; perhaps even the existence of such a judge would be of short duration."

The memorials were referred to a select committee, consisting of Foster of New Hampshire, Gerry of Massachusetts, Huntington of Connecticut, Lawrence of New York, Sinnickson of New Jersey, Hartley of Pennsylvania, and Parker of Virginia. From this committee Mr. Hartley made a report, manifestly well considered and carefully drawn up. In it the committee say that, from the nature of the matters contained in the memorials, they were induced to examine the powers vested in Congress under the present Constitution. Their conclusion was that the general government was prohibited from interfering with the slave-trade until the year 1808, that it was prohibited from interfering with the emancipation of slaves within the States, and that it had no right to interfere with the internal regulations of particular States. But they declared that Congress had power, if deemed advisable, to lay a tax of ten dollars on each slave imported; that it had the power to interdict the trade for foreign supply, and that it might regulate the home traffic in the interests of humanity; and that it might prohibit foreigners from fitting out vessels in American ports. The committee closed by informing the memorialists that, so far as Congress could do it constitutionally, it would aim to promote their humane objects " on the principles of justice, humanity, and good policy."

A report, however, so guarded and carefully restrained by the limitations of the Constitution, so moderate in tone and temper, was received with marked demonstrations of hostility by the representatives of the slaveholding class, and its consideration postponed for a week. When it was taken up, Mr. Smith of South Carolina moved to " negative the whole report." But it was taken up by paragraphs, and the same line of argument, already sketched, was pursued. The greatest violence and impatience, with denunciation and threats, came from South Carolina and Georgia, — then, as since, the self-constituted guardians and defenders of Southern interests and Southern honor. They applied the same epithets to the Quakers then which their successors have so freely used in regard to all antislavery reformers. They stigmatized

9

them, as they have Christians and philanthropists since, as hypocritical pretenders to a sanctity they did not possess, as factious intermeddlers with what did not concern them. They declared the compromises of the Constitution to be the only conditions on which the Union could be preserved ; and they sternly demanded that freedom of discussion on the subject of slavery should not be tolerated.

Among the champions of slavery, the most able and conspicuous, as well as rancorous and violent, were Smith, Tucker, and Burke of South Carolina, and Jackson and Baldwin of Georgia. Mr. Smith made an elaborate defence of slavery and the slave-trade on historical, scriptural, and humanitarian grounds. He denied the " horrors of the Middle Passage," and contended that slaves imported from Africa were benefited by the change, as they were here saved from a worse fate which awaited them in their native land. Freedom, however, was not without its true and steady defenders, — men who enunciated with great boldness and force the fundamental principles, the primal truths, not only of natural rights and obligation, but of Christian morality and duty. Trammelled, indeed, by those compromises which have always hampered the advocates of human rights under the Constitution, even the most conscientious and outspoken, they yet boldly denounced the system which had no sanction in reason or revelation. The most distinguished of these advocates were Vining of Delaware, and Scott and Boudinot of Pennsylvania.

This great and pregnant debate was closed on the 23d of March, when a substitute for the report was adopted in committee of the whole. On the suggestion of Mr. Madison, who desired to quiet the fears of the South, by showing that Congress claimed no power to prohibit the slave-trade till 1808, and no power to abolish slavery at all, the House, by a vote of twenty-nine to twenty-five, entered on the journal the report of the committee, and also the report of the committee of the whole, as amendments to that report. The amendments reported by the committee of the whole stood, therefore, as the judgment of the House.

By these resolutions the House of Representatives declared

that the importation of such persons as any of the States should admit could not be prohibited by Congress before 1808 ; that Congress had no power to interfere with emancipation or the treatment of slaves in the States ; but that it had authority to restrain the citizens of the United States from carrying on the slave-trade to supply foreigners with slaves, and that it had the power to make regulations for the humane treatment, on their passage, of slaves imported by citizens into States admitting such importations. Though these resolutions had not the authority of a legislative enactment, yet in all the subsequent conflicts growing out of the slavery question the doctrines therein embodied have been generally recognized as the true exposition of the Constitution, and of the powers of Congress touching that matter.

This debate on slavery was strikingly characteristic and significant. It clearly revealed in tone and temper, matter and manner, thought and language, that difference between the friends of freedom and the supporters of slavery, which has ever marked discussions growing out of their diversity of interests, views, feelings, and purposes. On the one side the debate was grave, dignified, and regardful of the rights of man and the authority of God ; on the other, it was flippant, contemptuous, and indifferent alike to the claims of humanity, the courtesies of debate, and the binding obligations of a Christian morality.

The abolition societies of Pennsylvania, New York, Rhode Island, Connecticut, and Virginia, in 1791, presented memorials calling upon Congress to exercise those powers which the House of Representatives had declared that Congress possessed, in the resolutions of the committee of the whole, which had been entered upon the journal. These memorials were referred to a special committee of which Mr. Benson of New York was made chairman. No action was taken by the committee. At the next session other memorials of a similar character were presented. But they were permitted to lie without action or reference.

In November, 1792, Mr. Ames presented a petition from Warner Mifflin, a Quaker gentleman of Delaware, setting forth the injustice of slavery and the wrongs of the slave. Two days afterward Mr. Steele of North Carolina called attention to the petition, and moved that it be taken from the table and returned to the petitioner, and that the record of its reception be erased. Smith of South Carolina denounced the petition as " the mere rant and rhapsody of a meddling fanatic, interlarded with texts of Scripture." He declared the real object of the petition to be to " create disunion among the States and to excite the most horrible insurrections." Declaring that petitions of that character were not calculated to ameliorate the condition of the slaves, but to excite a spirit of restlessness, which made greater securities necessary, he called upon the House to sustain the motion, and thus convince " this troublesome enthusiast, and others who might be disposed to communicate their ravings and wild effusions, that they would meet the treatment they justly deserve." Mr. Ames disapproved the object of the petitioners ; but defended the general right of petition, and justified, on that ground, his presentation of the memorial. The House sustained the motion to return the memorial to the petitioner ; and Mr. Steele then withdrew his motion to erase the record of its reception from the journal. This high-handed measure was a clear and palpable violation of the constitutional right of petition, a gross indignity to the petitioner, and an insult to a free people.

CHAPTER VI.

THE FUGITIVE SLAVE ACT OF 1793. — PROPOSED AMENDMENTS.

Bill for the Rendition of Fugitive Slaves. — Bill passed the Senate, — passed the House. — Petition of Free Colored Men to be protected against it. — Exciting Debate. — Memorial of Colored Men of Philadelphia. — Exciting and Violent Debate. — Disunion threatened by Mr. Rutledge. — Action of the House. — Further Legislation demanded. — Mr. Pindall's Bill. — Amendment by Mr. Rich. — Mr. Storrs' Amendment. — Debate on the Bill and Amendments. — Mr. Fuller's Amendments. — Bill passed the House, — passed the Senate, with Amendments. — House refused to take it up. — Mr. Wright's Resolution. — Bill reported by Judiciary Committee. — Debated. — Recommitted to a Select Committee. — Reported, but not acted on.

By their persistency the statesmen representing the Slave Power secured from the framers of the Constitution the provision for the rendition of fugitive slaves. Having obtained the incorporation of this provision into the fundamental law, they early and eagerly sought its enforcement.

In the Senate, in November, 1792, Mr. Johnston of North Carolina, Mr. Cabot of Massachusetts, and Mr. Read of Delaware were appointed a committee for the consideration of matters relating to fugitives from justice, and slaves escaping from their masters. The committee reported a bill in December, and on the 28th of the same month it was recommitted, and Mr. Taylor of Virginia and Mr. Sherman of Connecticut were added to the committee. On the 3d of January, 1793, Mr. Johnston reported the original bill, with amendments. It was considered several days, and passed without a division. On the 4th of February the House proceeded to its consideration, and the next day it passed by a vote of 48 to 7. Thus this act, which gave the slave-masters and their agents summary power to seize, hold, and return to slavery their fugitive bondmen, passed the Senate without a dissenting voice; and in the House there were found only seven members to record their votes against that dishonoring act, by authority of which so many inhuman and wicked deeds have been committed.

Under this Fugitive Slave Act of 1793 many arrests of persons alleged to have escaped from servitude were made, and much alarm among free persons of color was created. Many free negroes, especially in the States of Pennsylvania and Delaware, were kidnapped and sold into slavery. At the first session of the Fourth Congress a memorial was presented from the legislature of Delaware, asking the protection of the general government against this kidnapping. It was referred to the Committee on Commerce, which made a report asking for instructions.

In December, 1796, on motion of Mr. Swanwick of Pennsylvania, the report of the previous session was taken up for consideration. Mr. Coit of Connecticut, a member of the Committee of Commerce, thought the laws of the several States fully adequate without further provisions. He did not wish the United States to " intermeddle " in the case. To this Mr. Swanwick replied that the State laws were broken with impunity. He was for obliging masters of vessels when they took negroes on board to have certificates of their freedom. Mr. Murray of Maryland asked if the idea of preventing kidnapping meant the taking of " free negroes and selling them as slaves, or the taking of slaves and making them free ? " To this question Mr. Swanwick replied that it was " intended to prevent both evils." Any action of Congress was opposed by Mr. Smith of South Carolina, because the matter was a municipal regulation, which should be left to the State legislatures. The House was reminded by Mr. Smith of New Jersey that negroes had in many instances been taken upon ships at night, and then carried to the West Indies and other parts of the world and sold ; and that the existing State laws could not prevent that fraudulent practice.

Mr. Sitgreaves and Mr. Swanwick earnestly urged immediate action for the protection of unfortunate negroes and mulattoes exposed, by their color, to insult and injury. Mr. Smith of South Carolina feared that the " use of the word ' emanci-

pation ' " by Mr. Swanwick would spread alarm through some
of the States. He would drop the subject altogether. Mr.
Nicholas of Virginia expressed the hope that the subject
would not be dismissed; for if they of the Southern States
" unfortunately held slaves, they ought not to contribute to
make slaves of free men." After further debate the report
was recommitted to the Committee on Commerce; and on the
18th of January, 1797, Mr. Swanwick, by the instructions of
the committee, though against his own opinion, reported that
it was not expedient to interfere with the existing laws of the
States on that subject.

In January, 1797, Mr. Swanwick presented a petition from
persons of African descent, natives of North Carolina, who
had been emancipated and re-enslaved. These persons set
forth that they had been liberated " under the hand and seal
of conscientious masters," by authority of a law pronounced
constitutional; that another law had been enacted under which
men of " cruel disposition and void of principle " were seeking
to re-enslave them; that they were reduced to the necessity of
separating from their nearest and most tender connections, and
of seeking refuge in other parts of the country, always liable
to be seized and reduced to bondage again, under the provisions
of the Fugitive Slave Act. " To you only," they say, " under
God, can we apply, with any hope of effect, for redress of our
grievances."

Mr. Swanwick desired that the petition should be referred to
a select committee; but Mr. Blount of North Carolina hoped the
petition would not be received. A committee on the Fugitive
Slave Act had been appointed, and Mr. Thatcher of Massachusetts thought this petition should be referred to that committee. He asserted that they were free people, and had an
undoubted right to petition and be heard. Mr. Swanwick
animadverted on the atrocity of a reward of ten dollars offered
for one of them if taken alive, and fifty dollars if found dead,
and no questions to be asked. He denounced that " horrid reward," which gentlemen could not hear without a " shudder,"
as an encouragement to put an end to that man's life. Heath
and Madison of Virginia were in favor of letting the petition

lie on the table; but Mr. Rutherford of the same State favored the reference of the memorial to a committee, as the " great hardships " represented in the petition appealed closely to the nicest feelings of the heart, and he " hoped humanity would dictate a just decision." Mr. Gilbert of New Jersey thought the petition " laid claim to the humanity of the House "; but Mr. Smith of South Carolina was in favor of sealing it up and sending it back to the petitioners.

Mr. Thatcher said the Fugitive Slave Act had no authority over that set of men who claim the protection of that House, which ought " always to lean toward freedom." Though they could not give freedom to slaves, yet he hoped gentlemen would not refuse to lend their aid to secure freemen against tyrannical imposition. Mr. Varnum of Massachusetts said the petitioners had received injury under the provisions of the Fugitive Slave Act, as well as under the laws of North Carolina, and they had an undoubted right to the attention of the general government. If it should appear that they were free, and had received injuries under the Fugitive Slave Act, that Act ought to be amended. Mr. Kitchell of New Jersey maintained that the question was not whether they were or were not slaves, but whether a committee should inquire into the improper enforcement of the Fugitive Slave Act in their case. But the House refused to receive the petition, thirty-three voting for it and fifty against it.

In December, 1799, Robert Waln of Pennsylvania presented a petition from colored men in Philadelphia, praying for the revision of the Fugitive Slave Act and the laws relative to the slave-trade, and for the adoption of such measures as should in the course of time emancipate their brethren. Its reference was earnestly opposed by Mr. Rutledge of South Carolina, who contemptuously observed that the gentlemen who formerly came forward with their petitions had now put them into the hands of the "black gentlemen." These petitioners reminded the House that black people were in slavery. He " thanked God that they were; if they were not, dreadful would be the consequences." Mr. Smilie of Pennsylvania said that these colored people were " a part of the human species, equally capable of suffering and enjoying, equally the objects of attention, and they had a claim to be heard."

Harrison Gray Otis had never seen a petition presented under a more dangerous aspect; and he opposed the reference. Henry Lee of Virginia, father of Robert E. Lee, the rebel general, would have the petition returned to the gentleman who presented it, " as Congress had no power over slavery but to protect it." Mr. Brown of Rhode Island hoped that Northern men would see the impropriety of encouraging slaves to come from Southern States to " become thieves and vagabonds." He was not a slaveholder, but he considered " slaves as much property as a farm or a ship." John Randolph, who had just entered Congress, desired that the action of the House should be so decided as to deter persons from petitioning on that subject thereafter ; and Mr. Christie of Maryland hoped the petition would go " under the table, rather than on it." He was in favor of taking up the Fugitive Act, and, instead of weakening it, " making it stronger." Robert Goodloe Harper thought the temper of revolt was more perceptible among the slaves ; and Mr. Jones of Georgia hoped the petition would be treated with " the contempt it merited, and thrown under the table."

In the course of the debate Mr. Thatcher fitly characterized the remarks of his colleague, Mr. Otis, " as pitiful, mean, virulent." Mr. Edmond of Connecticut said it was unjust in the House, instead of giving a patient attention, to treat the complaints of the petitioners with " an inattention that passion alone could dictate." It was then proposed by Mr. Goode of Virginia that the petition should receive the pointed disapprobation of the House. To this proposition Mr. Thatcher replied that this was the first time he had ever known a petition, or a part of a petition, to receive the marked disapprobation of the House. If a petition in favor of objects so worthy was not heard, it would be " a national indignity." Mr. Rutledge, perhaps the ablest, certainly the most devoted and outspoken of the champions of the slaveholding interest, emphatically proclaimed that the abolition of slavery would never take place. " There is," he said, " one alternative which

10

will save us from it, — but that alternative I deprecate very much, — that is, that we are able to take care of ourselves; and, if driven to it, we will take care of ourselves." The House then resolved that those parts of the petition praying Congress to legislate on subjects from which the government is precluded by the Constitution had a tendency to create disquiet and jealousy, and ought therefore to receive no countenance or encouragement. This resolution received the votes of eighty-five members, the inflexible Thatcher alone voting in the negative.

This hesitating and timid action seems a lame and impotent conclusion of a debate so imbued with the spirit of humanity, justice, and freedom on the one part, though revealing on the other an utter disregard of the rights of man and the claims of Christian morality. But is it, after all, when viewed in the light of the compromises of the Constitution, a matter of surprise? The concessions then made were, and ever have been, the weak and vulnerable points in all the conflicts between freedom and oppression. The framers of the fundamental law, avoiding the name of slavery, admitted into that instrument "the guilty fantasy that man can hold property in man." The slaveholders in their struggles ever claimed that " it was so nominated in the bond," and persistently demanded their " pound of flesh." And so the integrity, honor, and even the Christianity of the nation were invoked, — and too often successfully, — to sanction the schemes of inhumanity and the injustice of men determined to make the most of advantages surrendered by those fatal concessions.

Severe as were the provisions of this act, complaints were continually made by slave-masters that it did not afford adequate facilities for the recapture of their escaped slaves. More stringent provisions and a more rigid enforcement of the law were still demanded.

In the House, in December, 1817, Mr. Pindall of Virginia, Mr. Beecher of Ohio, and Mr. Anderson of Kentucky were appointed a committee to devise more effectual means for the reclamation of fugitive slaves. A bill for this purpose was reported; and the House, on the 26th of January, 1818, pro-

ceeded to its consideration. Its provisions were explained by
the chairman of the committee. It was moved by Mr. Rich
of Vermont so to amend it as to prevent the transportation of
any person claimed as a slave without taking such person
before a court of record and furnishing sufficient proof that
such person was a slave, and the property of the person
attempting to remove him, under a penalty of ten thousand
dollars. Mr. Storrs of New York moved to amend the bill by
substituting, in lieu of the amendment of Mr. Rich, a new
section, providing that, if any person, without a colorable
claim, should procure a certificate or warrant to arrest or
transport any person not held as a slave, he should himself
be punished by imprisonment not exceeding fifteen years, or
by fine not exceeding five thousand dollars. Mr. Pindall
united with Mr. Storrs in supporting his amendment, and Mr.
Rich vindicated his own amendment on the ground of the
enormity of the crime of kidnapping; but Mr. Storrs's amendment was adopted by a large majority.

It was maintained by Mr. Claggett of New Hampshire that
existing laws secured to the claimants all the rights that the
Constitution guaranteed to them. If any legislation was necessary, it was to restrain the claimants from the abuse of power.
Mr. Pindall maintained that the duty of delivering up fugitive
slaves was imposed on the States, and that Congress could by
law define and regulate the action of State officers in the per-
formance of that duty. Mr. Fuller of Massachusetts moved
to strike out the first section of the bill, because it transcended
the provisions of the Constitution; and Mr. Strong spoke earnestly in opposition to the measure. Mr. Cobb of Georgia vindicated the rights of the holders of slaves as "inalienable and
inviolable." Mr. Hopkinson of Pennsylvania thought that freemen might be apprehended, unless proper means of redress
were provided. John Holmes of Massachusetts, afterward senator from Maine, expressed the opinion that the bill could be so
worded as to be "unobjectionable" to any one. The nature
of slave property, its evils, and the rights of its possessors were
stated, defined, and illustrated by Mr. Clay. Mr. Baldwin of
Pennsylvania, a native of Connecticut, a lawyer of eminence,

and afterward a judge of the Supreme Court, maintained that the Constitution conferred upon Congress the power so to legislate as to afford the fullest protection to the holders of slaves. The amendment proposed by Mr. Fuller was rejected.

It was then moved by Mr. Rich to recommit the bill to the committee to which was referred the memorial of the Quakers of Baltimore, to report such action as would protect the free people of color. The motion to recommit was defeated without a division. John Sergeant of Pennsylvania, one of the most distinguished advocates and statesmen of that day, then moved to amend the bill by empowering the judges of the State in which the person should be arrested, rather than the judges of the State from which it was alleged he had escaped, to determine whether such person owed service or labor. But this amendment was defeated by a large majority. Mr. Rich offered several other amendments to guard the rights of freemen, but they were rejected. It was then, by a large majority, ordered to a third reading.

The passage of the bill was strenuously opposed by Benjamin Adams of Massachusetts, because it contained provisions " dangerous to liberty and to the safety of free persons of color "; and Mr. Livermore of New Hampshire opposed it because it provided that alleged fugitives were not to be identified until they reached the State where the persons claiming them resided. This provision would expose free persons of color to be dragged from one part of the country to another. Jonathan Mason of Massachusetts — who had served in the Senate from 1800 to 1803, and who, though a Federalist, had been elected to the House over Mr. Ritchie, son-in-law of Harrison Gray Otis, by a few Federalists and by the Democratic party, and who afterward betrayed his constituents by voting for the Missouri Compromise — spoke at length in approval of the measure. He thought the tribunals of the South would decide more correctly than those of the North. So great was the leaning against slavery in Massachusetts, that in ninety-nine cases out of a hundred juries would decide in favor of the fugitive. He did not wish, by denying just facilities for the recovery of fugitive slaves, to have the town where he lived " infested with the runaways of the South."

Milton Keynes UK
Ingram Content Group UK Ltd.
UKHW022254271123
433389UK00005B/235

9 781016 178990